ITIL® V3 Small-scale Implementation

London: TSO

Published by TSO (The Stationery Office) and available from:

Online
www.tsoshop.co.uk

Mail, Telephone, Fax & E-mail
TSO
PO Box 29, Norwich, NR3 1GN
Telephone orders/General enquiries: 0870 600 5522
Fax orders: 0870 600 5533
E-mail: customer.services@tso.co.uk
Textphone 0870 240 3701

TSO@Blackwell and other Accredited Agents

Customers can also order publications from:
TSO Ireland
16 Arthur Street, Belfast BT1 4GD
Tel 028 9023 8451 Fax 028 9023 5401

First published 2009

ISBN 9780113310784

Printed in the United Kingdom for The Stationery Office
N6113802   c17   08/09   19585   175

Contents

List of figures

List of tables

Foreword

There is some evidence to suggest that people see the adoption of ITIL® as a massive undertaking that is only worthwhile for a major organization which is supported by significant information technology. I believe, however, that the practices encompassed by ITIL can provide help whatever the size of the organization, which points to an obvious communications gap.

I tend to think of ITIL as if it was an approach to mountaineering – it helps prepare you for the climb up Mount Everest. It identifies the skills, infrastructure and support systems that need to be in place to take you on such a journey. Equally, if you want to climb (or walk) up a much smaller mountain, you would be foolish not to make some preparations – indeed, you should follow the same principles as for the trip in the Himalayas, recognizing that the size and the scale of the task are different.

Continuing with the mountain analogy, the core ITIL guidance can most easily be understood if you view it as the route map necessary to reach the top of the highest IT service management mountain – Mount Everest. If you wish to scale down your operations and simply prepare to ascend a more modest peak, then this is the guide for you.

I trust you will find the book enjoyable, informative and useful when planning to scale your own IT service management mountain.

Frances Scarff

Frances Scarff

Head of Best Management Practice, OGC

Acknowledgements

Authors

Sharon Taylor	Aspect Group Inc.
Ivor Macfarlane	IBM

This publication is the third version (V3) of the original ITIL book published in 1995 (*ITIL Practices in Small IT Units*), and so it is appropriate to recognize the significant contributions to that original product made by Jenny Ellwood-Wade and Tony Jenkins.

Reviewers

The Office of Government Commerce (OGC) and The Stationery Office (TSO) would like to thank itSMF for their help in the quality assurance of this publication. TSO would also like to thank those people who have generously donated their time in reviewing this new edition. These reviewers include:

Janaki Chakravarthy	Infosys Technologies Limited, India
Robert Falkowitz	Concentric Circle Consulting, Switzerland
Matiss Horodishtiano	Amdocs Ltd, Israel
Dave Jones	Pink Elephant, UK
Kirstie Magowan	Verso Solutions, New Zealand
Christian F. Nissen	CFN PEOPLE (formerly Itilligence), Denmark
Sunit Prakash	Independent, New Zealand
Stuart Rance	Hewlett Packard, UK
John Sowerby	DHL IT Services, USA

Thanks are still due to all of those who contributed to and reviewed the previous edition of this book, *ITIL Small-scale Implementation* (TSO, 2005). These people include:

J. Andrew Atencio	USA
Janaki Chakravarthy	India
Alison Cartlidge	UK
Karen Ferris	Australia
Chris Jones	Australia
Christian F. Nissen	Denmark
Doug Read	UK
Sue Shaw	UK
Jan van Bon	The Netherlands

Harnessing the power of ITIL in small and medium-sized businesses

1

1 Harnessing the power of ITIL in small and medium-sized businesses

IT service management (ITSM) industry analysts predict that over the next five years, small and medium-sized businesses (SMBs) will be the largest growth sector in the world. This entrepreneurial segment of business is capitalizing on its strengths – agility, speed to market, flexible business models and the control that major enterprises often cannot match.

The risks to longevity are high in the SMB market and only those who are prepared for dynamic and rapid change in market conditions will survive. The positioning of ITSM within these organizations is a key success factor in their survival. A crucial ingredient in this strategy is the adoption and use of the ITIL service management practices. ITSM vendors have responded with product and service strategies targeted directly at this market space.

Most IT organizations share some level of commonality. SMBs, for example, have constraints and requirements just as large organizations do. They are accountable to their business customers to provide value. But in many SMBs, there are unique opportunities and constraints which set them apart from large organizations.

This publication is for the SMB. It is intended to help small or medium-sized organizations reap the power and benefits of ITIL while removing the constraints of a large-scale implementation.

It is equally important to note that this publication is **not** about ways to shortcut ITIL by adopting selected lifecycle stages or elements and eliminating others. Part of ITIL's strength is the integrated, holistic service lifecycle. For some organizations, scaling these practices will make their use efficient, cost-effective and enable the adoption of best practice within an SMB context.

This publication is based upon a simple truth: ITIL can offer guidance that will help every size and type of company improve their IT service management performance. The scalability of implementation is the key to success. Within the following chapters we offer some explanation of why and how smaller organizations are different, and offer some ideas and techniques that might help smaller ITSM organizations to improve the quality of the service they deliver to their customers and users.

This publication considers how the circumstances of delivering effective IT service management are affected by the situations and constraints that typically occur within a small organization, and how to get good results quickly by adapting the ITIL advice to circumstance.

ITIL in an ITSM best-practice context

2

2 ITIL in an ITSM best-practice context

ITIL does not stand alone but fits into an ITSM best-practice context (see Figure 2.1). Regardless of size, every organization should have a blend of ITSM practices to ensure a holistic approach. Running an IT organization is like running any business. The need for management controls and performance indicators exists from the strategic right through to the operational layers.

Some common ITSM control layers in use today include:

- **Strategy**

  IT governance   This is the responsibility of the board of directors and executive management as an integral part of enterprise governance. Typically it consists of management, organizational structures and processes

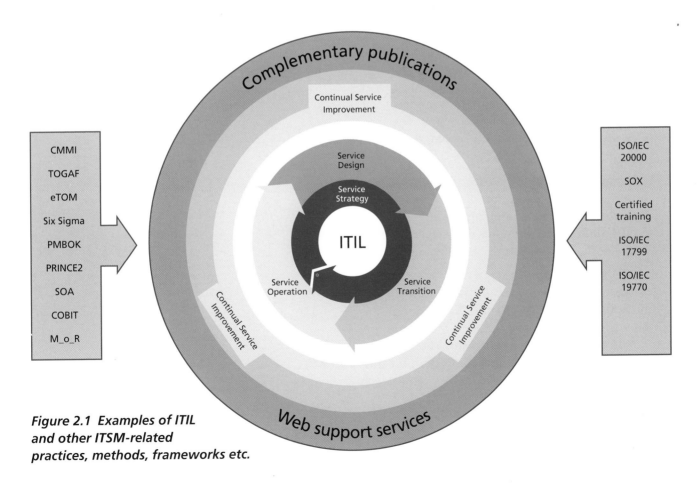

Figure 2.1 Examples of ITIL and other ITSM-related practices, methods, frameworks etc.

to ensure that IT sustains and extends the organizational strategies and objectives

■ **Management**

Standards   National or international standards related to IT practice and systems management are available in the industry. These include ISO/IEC 20000:2005, 27001:2005 and 17799:2005

Frameworks   Lifecycle practices, processes, functions and workflows are combined in frameworks for management such as ITIL. These will often serve as the base for practice competence to enable compliance to standards or governance

■ **Performance**

Models   Measurement models such as maturity models assess organizational maturity against practice characteristics. Scorecards are often used to compartmentalize different aspects of organizational capability that refined performance measures can be applied to

■ **Operations**

Processes   Generally derived from frameworks, these are the daily execution practices often developed, maintained and improved in response to the requirements of disciplines such as service management, project management or risk management.

Experts are often asked which of these control layers should be considered. There is no right or wrong answer, but generally a blend of a few is a common approach. Later in this publication, guidance is offered on a balanced approach for the SMB.

The ITIL service lifecycle

3

3 The ITIL service lifecycle

3.1 THE ITIL VALUE PROPOSITION

All high-performing service providers share similar characteristics. This is not coincidence. There are specific capabilities inherent in their success that they demonstrate consistently. A core capability is their strategy. If you were to ask a high-achieving service provider what makes them distinctive from their competitors, they would tell you that it is their intrinsic understanding of how they provide value to their customers. They understand the customers' business objectives and the role they play in enabling those objectives to be met. A closer look would reveal that their ability to do this does not come from reacting to customer needs, but from predicting them through preparation, analysis and examining customer usage patterns. The intimacy that an SMB organization enjoys with its customers makes this an excellent strength for differentiation and sustaining a long-term, trusted partnership between the SMB and its customers.

The potential for this intimacy is an inherent feature of smaller organizations – derived from the ability of those controlling the organization to also be closely involved with customers and aware of both business strategy and operations. As an organization grows, this ability will fade, and organizations for which this is critical may – correctly – choose to remain as SMBs. A key message of this situation is that an SMB should not be viewed as just a step on the way to growing large for a successful company. It can be – and often is – a deliberate, successful and correct ongoing strategy for a successful business.

The next significant characteristic is the systematic use of service management practices that are responsive, consistent and measurable, and which define the provider's quality in the eyes of its customers. These practices provide stability and predictability and permeate the service provider's culture.

The final characteristic is the provider's ability to analyse continuously and fine-tune service provision to maintain stable, reliable yet adaptive and responsive services that allow the customer to focus on their business without concern for IT service reliability.

3.2 THE ITIL SERVICE MANAGEMENT PRACTICES

ITIL is an integrated set of publications which offer best-practice guidance applicable to all sizes and types of organizations providing services to a business. Each publication addresses capabilities having direct impact on a service provider's performance. The structure of the core practice takes the form of a service lifecycle. It is iterative and multidimensional. It ensures organizations are set up to leverage capabilities in one area for learning and improvement in others. The core is expected to provide structure, stability and strength to service management capabilities with durable principles, methods and tools. This serves to protect investments and provide the necessary basis for measurement, learning and improvement.

The guidance in ITIL can be adapted for use in various business environments and organizational strategies. This publication is one element of the ITIL complementary guidance which will provide the flexibility necessary to implement the core guidance in a diverse range of environments. Practitioners can select complementary guidance as needed to provide traction for the core in a given business context, in much the same way as tyres are selected based on the type of vehicle, purpose and road conditions. This is to increase the durability and portability of knowledge assets and to protect investments in service management capabilities.

3.3 SERVICE MANAGEMENT

Service management is more than just a set of capabilities. It is also a professional practice supported by an extensive body of knowledge, experience and skills. A global community of individuals and organizations in the public and private sectors fosters its growth and maturity. Formal schemes exist for the education, training and certification of practising organizations, and individuals influence its quality. Industry best practices, academic research and formal standards contribute to its intellectual capital and draw from it.

The origins of service management are in traditional service businesses such as airlines, banks, hotels, phone companies and healthcare. Its practice has grown with the adoption by IT organizations of a service-oriented approach to managing IT applications, infrastructure and processes. Solutions to business problems and support for business models, strategies and operations are increasingly in the form of services. The popularity of shared services and outsourcing has contributed to the increase in the number of organizations who are service providers, including internal organizational units. This in turn has

strengthened the practice of service management and at the same time imposed greater challenges upon it.

3.4 WHAT IS A SERVICE?

ITIL definition of a service

A service is a means of delivering value to customers by facilitating outcomes customers want to achieve without the ownership of specific costs and risks.

There are a variety of contexts in which the definition of a service can be expanded, but as a basic concept, service is the means of delivering value, and no matter how your organization chooses to describe a service, this must be at the heart of what defines a service.

Without an understanding of the services received by the customer, a service provider cannot practise meaningful service management. Some, or even most, of the processes that support service management may be present, but genuine service management must rest on knowledge of services. This does not demean the importance of the supporting processes, nor belittle the amount of effort, skill, knowledge and management they require. But proper awareness of services allows service management as a whole to integrate and deliver the fruits of the hard work in a fashion that meets customer needs.

The choice to use a service is driven by the relative costs and risks that would be inherent in delivering the service output internally instead. For example, most people would see the cost benefits of using a hotel as outweighing the benefits involved in buying an apartment and therefore a fuller degree of control over nature and standards of accommodation. Similarly, however good a service delivered by a rental car company may be, as the frequency and distance of travel increases, so almost everyone would see the advantages of switching to car ownership – taking on board also the risks and overheads that were previously the responsibility of the service provider.

Establishing the essential descriptive and positional factors of services is therefore the obvious starting point. The two key elements are knowledge of:

- Identity, role and scope of the direct customers of the service provider
- Services received by customers (what are they, and who delivers them).

The ITIL service lifecycle
– core of practice

4

4   The ITIL service lifecycle – core of practice

It is assumed that readers of this publication are familiar with the basic concepts and principles within the ITIL service lifecycle core practices to at least an introductory level similar to that of *The Official Introduction to the ITIL Service Lifecycle* (TSO, 2007) and/or the ITIL Foundation qualification. The following excerpts are from the core practice guidance focusing on the key areas of context.

4.1   ADOPTING A SERVICE LIFECYCLE APPROACH

Until recently, the traditional view of ITSM centred on a process-centric approach. Advances in best practices have shifted toward using processes to drive activities through a service lifecycle.

4.2   THE ITIL SERVICE LIFECYCLE

The service lifecycle (see Figure 4.1) contains five elements, each of which relies on service principles, processes and functions, organization, roles and performance measures. The service lifecycle uses a hub and spoke design, with service strategy at the hub, service design, transition and operation as the revolving lifecycle stages, and anchored by continual service improvement. Each part of the lifecycle exerts influence on the others and relies on the others for inputs and feedback. In this way, a constant set of checks and balances throughout the service lifecycle ensures that as business demands change with business need, the services can adapt and respond effectively to them.

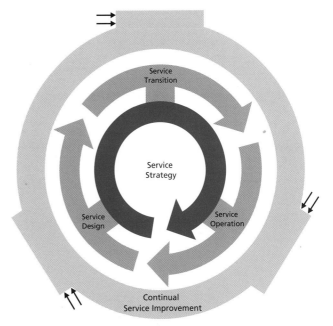

Figure 4.1 The ITIL service lifecycle

At the heart of the service lifecycle is the key principle – **all services must provide measurable value to business objectives and outcomes**. ITIL service management focuses on business value as its prime objective. Each practice revolves around ensuring that everything a service provider does to manage IT services for the business customer can be measured and quantified in terms of business value. This has become extremely important today, as IT organizations must operate as businesses in order to demonstrate a clear return on investment and equate service performance with business value to the customer.

4.3 FUNCTIONS AND PROCESSES ACROSS THE LIFECYCLE

Functions are units of organizations specialized to perform certain types of work and responsible for specific outcomes. They are self-contained, with capabilities and resources necessary to their performance and outcomes. Capabilities include work methods internal to the functions. Functions have their own body of knowledge, which accumulates from experience. They provide structure and stability to organizations.

4.3.1 Functions

Functions typically define roles and the associated authority and responsibility for specific performance and outcomes. Coordination between functions through shared processes is a common pattern in organization design. Functions tend to optimize their work methods locally to focus on assigned outcomes. Poor coordination between functions combined with an inward focus leads to functional silos that hinder alignment and feedback critical to the success of the organization as a whole. Process models help avoid this problem with functional hierarchies by improving cross-functional coordination and control. Well-defined processes can improve productivity within and across functions.

4.3.2 Processes

Processes are examples of closed-loop systems because they provide change and transformation towards a goal, and use feedback for self-reinforcing and self-corrective action. It is important to consider the entire process or how one process fits into another (see Figure 4.2).

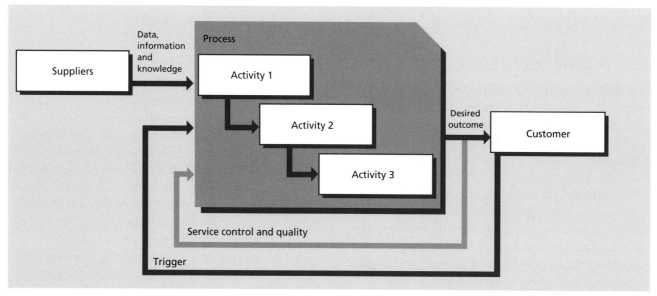

Figure 4.2 Process architecture

Process definitions describe actions, dependencies and sequence. Processes have the following characteristics:

- They are measurable and are performance-driven. Managers want to measure cost, quality and other variables while practitioners are concerned with duration and productivity
- They have specific results. The reason a process exists is to deliver a specific result. This result must be individually identifiable and countable
- They deliver measurable output. Every process delivers its primary results to a customer or stakeholder. Customers or stakeholders may be internal or external to the organization but the process must meet their expectations
- They respond to a specific event. While a process may be ongoing or iterative, it should be traceable to a specific trigger.

4.3.3 Resources and capabilities

In an SMB, with the likelihood of a set of services tightly focused on the organization's business goals, establishing and maintaining appropriate resources and capabilities is essential. The resources are the more tangible, more easily identified and measured element – finance, information, infrastructure etc. SMBs have traditionally struggled to get enough resources, although by no means is this problem restricted to SMBs.

Capabilities are developed over time, and relevant capabilities are matched to the business's needs. The more intimate nature of an SMB makes the acquisition of capabilities even more essential – and the likely volatility of many SMBs makes their maintenance to ensure continued relevance even more critical. The key aspect of appropriate capabilities is that they match the customer's situation, requirements, attitudes and way of

working, so capabilities will vary considerably from organization to organization and over time as organizations grow, mature or change in other ways. However, some aspects that might be especially relevant in SMBs could include:

- Experience in the market sector
- Shared culture (and therefore aims and attitudes) with the rest of the organization
- Flexibility and adaptability.

These kinds of capabilities are unlikely to be available to the business from any other source and can provide real added value for the internal IT supplier, and it is often worth their while to make these – and the value that they do indeed add – as visible as possible to the customer. One way to achieve this might be for the supplier to be seen to offer fast and flexible support to business strategy as well as constructive and relevant proactive input to that strategy.

4.3.4 Specialization and coordination across the lifecycle

Specialization and coordination are necessary in the lifecycle approach. Feedback and control between the functions and processes within and across the elements of the lifecycle make this possible. The dominant pattern in the lifecycle is the sequential progress starting from service strategy (SS) through service delivery (SD), service transition (ST), service operation (SO) and back to service strategy through continual service improvement (CSI). That, however, is not the only pattern of action. Every element of the lifecycle provides points for feedback and control.

The combination of multiple perspectives allows greater flexibility and control across environments and situations. The lifecycle approach mimics the reality of most organizations where effective management requires the use of multiple control perspectives. Those responsible for the design, development and improvement of processes for service management can adopt a process-based control perspective. Those responsible for managing agreements, contracts and services may be better served by a lifecycle-based control perspective with distinct phases. Both these control perspectives benefit from systems thinking. Each

control perspective can reveal patterns that may not be apparent from the other.

4.3.5 Feedback throughout the service lifecycle

The strength of the ITIL service lifecycle rests upon continual feedback throughout each stage of the lifecycle. This feedback ensures that service optimization is managed from a business

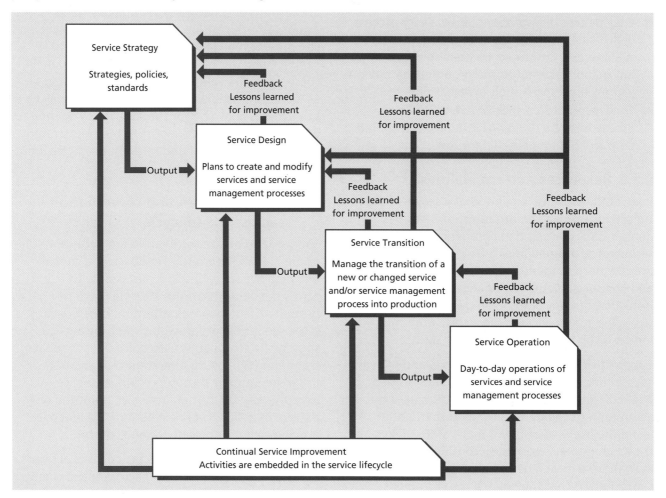

Figure 4.3 Continual feedback loop

perspective and is measured in terms of the value business derives from services at any point in time through the service lifecycle. The ITIL service lifecycle is non-linear in design. At every point in the service lifecycle, monitoring, assessment and feedback flows between each stage of the lifecycle drive decisions about the need for minor course corrections or major service improvement initiatives. Figure 4.3 illustrates some examples of the continual feedback system built into the ITIL service lifecycle.

Profile of a small to
medium-sized business

5

5 Profile of a small to medium-sized business

If you think of any organization as a community of people, you see that each has distinct nuances and interactions. If you then change the magnitude of the community, you see those nuances and interactions change dramatically. There are significant differences between the characteristics of small and large organizations.

Consider the size of IT organizations from a village and city perspective, and the differences between them. These differences can be summarized by comparing the SMB organization to a village and the larger organization to a city. The most important indication from this analogy is not about size or any actual characteristics of human villages or cities – it is that the important differences are based on attitudes and behaviour, and upon the familiarity with the circumstances, opportunities and constraints that come from the immediate environment we live or work in. The relative merits of village and city life have long been debated elsewhere (see *The Tale of Johnny Town-Mouse*, Beatrix Potter, 1918). The important point is that there are fundamental differences which have to be recognized and accounted for. Different kinds of approaches and solutions are required in each case.

There are typical characteristics of a small to medium-sized business that come to mind for most of us:

- A small number of staff
- Usually operating in few locations
- A small number of users.

There are also other characteristics, common to many SMBs, that influence their mode of operation and shape the pressures they must work under:

- Low ratio of IT staff to users
- Limited fiscal resources
- Small budgets and staff numbers
- Disproportionate IT support organizations, e.g. support-to-users ratio much lower than the industry norm
- Minimal disposable budgets to investigate new initiatives
- Restricted time frames in which to demonstrate improvement
- Restricted collaboration from colleagues and customers.

We tend to think that 'small' relates to the number of staff in an organization, and while that is often the defining factor, other characteristics will also cause an IT organization to be considered and behave as a small business, such as:

- An IT organization within a large company that has limited means either financially or technologically
- A stable organization with significant resistance to innovation where IT is not seen as a source of innovation or frequent change.

5.1 INFORMAL CULTURE

One way of addressing these differences is to compare the interactions among the staff (through which many of the service management processes are delivered) with those that take place in society.

Whatever the technology, or even the number of staff, SMBs can be expected to share common characteristics which differentiate them from larger organizations.

Perhaps the most obvious and immediately noticeable difference between small and large IT organizations is culture. Within an SMB, there is often a relatively informal atmosphere, as people know the majority of staff within the organization, rather than just those in their small segment of a larger and complex interactive structure. Staff in an SMB are more aware of their collective abilities, likely reactions, attitudes, prejudices and perspectives etc.

This contrasts with the environments of larger IT organizations, where procedures and formality are much more prevalent, and submissions and requests are more impersonal, required to address wider and perhaps conflicting goals across large organizations rather than individuals' views. However, informality is not always a good thing. It can result in serious risks, especially where ITIL disciplines such as configuration management or change management are concerned. Some degree of formality is a necessary part of managing; without it, SMB organizations can lose control over essential aspects of the service, with very costly results.

5.2 TEAM SPIRIT

In a small organization (whether it be an IT organization, a sports team or any other group working to deliver a common purpose) members are likely to see themselves as members of a single team, with common goals.

This sense of unity fades as the organization grows in size. Here the environment is large enough to allow a number of internal teams to develop, with potential rivalry between the different IT branches. This can quickly block collaboration, whereas in small organizations the team spirit is likely to expand beyond the walls of traditional ITSM and enable closer collaboration with testing, application development, procurement and other associated processes.

5.3 QUICK COMMUNICATION

Good communication in a small organization is almost inevitable since each person will be responsible for several roles. When there is a communication of common interest, it will spread across the entire organization quickly – often driven by gossip and social traffic.

This can encourage strong informal communications between the IT organization and the business. These links help to ensure that things are done with the minimum number of complications, but can also lead to things happening without sufficient consideration, consultation and documentation, or even on occasion without financial or management approval.

In larger organizations, on the other hand, communication is almost always a problem. Everything must be formally recorded and procedures are needed to make sure all the right people are kept in touch with each other. While small organizations do need to carefully document and record initiatives and outcomes, the complexity and tendency for omission or confusion is greatly increased by the complexity inherent in a larger organization.

5.4   RESPONSIVENESS

SMB organizations can be very responsive, developing and amending plans and procedures as they go. The sheer inertia that goes with large staff numbers is mostly absent, allowing for fast decisions in an environment small enough to canvass everybody's views within a day. This has the benefits of:

- **Allowing initiatives to get started with less planning**   This will be interpreted by the customer as a more caring and responsive IT service, so long as the initiatives are useful to the customer
- **Tailoring ideas during a project or service**   Changes are easier because the decision-makers are more likely to be available and because the staff involved are much more likely to know the requirements and abilities of the rest of the IT organization. Thus, changes are more likely to be:
  - Made quickly, for example, within a day
  - Accepted by other staff
  - Tailored to the customers' needs
- **Tailoring services to small numbers of staff**   Providing a service to thousands of users across a large company inevitably means that the users see it as centrally organized and imposed. The SMB organization working within a small company has more chance to personalize its services. This can be especially valuable when there is a diverse range of users and customers, for example R&D groups.

5.5   FLEXIBILITY

Small organizations can react to changes and new ideas very quickly. Negotiating, agreeing and – above all – delivering changes and ideas is easier as a smaller number of staff means there are plenty of shortcuts available.

If something needs to be discussed or decided, all the major players can probably be brought together in the same room at the same time. New ideas are more likely to at least get attention, and probably receive support. Again, this ease of agreement is often reflected in the ability to implement quickly, and to adapt and actually deliver a change rather than pause to involve myriad stakeholders before adaptation and completion. This can also bring risks, but the risk/benefit assessment and re-assessment requirement will usually be a quicker operation within a smaller organization.

Also, small organizations can dare to do things which larger organizations cannot because they can reach decision-makers and because, since everyone knows each other, less preliminary work is required in preparing and justifying initiatives.

5.6   UNDERSTANDING THE BUSINESS

The smaller an organization, the more likely it is that those working within it can clearly see the supply and process chain that delivers the organization's business products or services. This extends to the ITSM staff who, aware of their role in the overall organization, have an advantage in tailoring their work to better fit the business needs.

5.7   LACK OF SPECIALISTS

All organizations have tasks that require a degree of specialization, i.e. the kind of knowledge that comes from focusing much of the time on a small field of expertise. Even small organizations require specialists to deliver key functions. These experts should know about their customers' business practices and the latest developments in relevant IT. However, the inevitable restrictions upon the range of proficiency the small organization can support means that any specialists must be carefully tuned to the organization's needs.

Within a larger organization, in contrast, there is more scope for people to concentrate exclusively on one specific area, working in relative isolation from the rest of the organization and the business. This may have implications for training staff, especially when they face moving from a large IT organization into a smaller one, something occurring more frequently as large organizations fragment under the pressures of outsourcing, downsizing and user empowerment.

5.8   RELIANCE ON INDIVIDUALS

Within SMBs, the reliance on one person to know things and be the local expert is inevitable. Only where there is a major risk to business viability can the cost of training extra people be justified. This leads to the establishment of 'heroes', individuals who are the only people with the skill and/or knowledge to deal with incidents, situations or opportunities that are likely to arise. While heroes inevitably deal quickly and competently with things when needed, during their absence potentially critical functions may not be possible.

It is probably wise to accept that there will be such heroes, but to take steps to make the best of the situation:

■ Try to plan properly for times when they will be absent from the office

■ Document their existence, identify risks and frequently confirm that those risks remain acceptable

■ Ensure that these experts stay up to date in their field of expertise, attending relevant training events and conferences

■ Do what you can to retain them in the organization through incentives and job satisfaction.

SMBs have to be aware that staff can leave suddenly for a variety of unavoidable reasons, and organizations must make sure that functions can survive the departure of any one individual. So, while formal communication between separate sections is not usually necessary, it is vital to record what has been decided and what has been done.

5.9   NOWHERE TO HIDE

A small environment means that if things go wrong, there are fewer options for solving problems. For example, when there are personality clashes, there is little that can be done to prevent them from causing damage.

On the other hand, if there are personality clashes in larger organizations, staff can be moved around to minimize disruption and conflict. Larger organizations also have the ability to organize people into meaningful groups or sections, allowing them to gain expertise in a particular aspect of IT.

5.10   LIMITED KNOWLEDGE

Related to its relative lack of specialists, the SMB is also likely to have gaps in its knowledge base, since a few people cannot know everything.

To make the most of the skills that are available, small organizations often have to combine several roles (even potentially separate job functions) within a single post, using staff as generalists rather than specialists. Another way of maximizing skills is to let the skills that are actually available define the structure of the organization. This can be more efficient than trying to create a structure around a theoretical requirement. As staff change, the structure can be reorganized.

Where skills are not available in-house, small organizations can make use of services from third-party suppliers, such as outside consultants, rather than trying to cope with their own limited resources. This reduces the specialist skills required within the organization, and provides those skills economically for the short time they are needed. This is effectively a decision based on financial considerations.

For the larger IT organization, staff skills and experts are readily available, providing cover for absence and a second opinion on difficult questions.

5.11 HIGH ORGANIZATION COSTS

Small IT organizations are not in a position to benefit on their own from the economies of scale which may be available to larger organizations. This means that the total cost to the organization of employing and supporting each member of IT staff will be higher, reflecting, among other things:

- Higher training and skill levels – since specialists may not be sustainable over a longer term, staff need to have knowledge of more areas and each will need a wider range of expertise
- Higher relative costs of essential software tools

- Cross-training can be more costly to a small organization, but may well be critically important in protecting business services.

The cost of IT per user is also likely to be higher, not only for these reasons, but also because:

- Hardware and software licence costs will be relatively higher
- More consultancy will be required (although if funds for consultancy are not available this would result in lower service levels being delivered).

Generally, higher costs to operate SMB organizations add to the burden of constraints from an overall ITSM perspective.

5.12 PER CAPITA COMPLEXITY

It is a common misunderstanding that small means simple. In fact, many tasks are more complex in an SMB. Standard configurations are less likely with small diverse customer communities, and a higher percentage of users are likely to use more customized technologies. This can precipitate more complexity and variety of:

- Incidents
- Configuration items (CIs) and configuration item relationships
- Networking software and hardware
- Applications, locations and usability issues.

5.13 LIMITED OPPORTUNITIES FOR CAREER GROWTH

Within SMBs IT staff may face limited opportunities for career growth, or may perceive it so, since the roles are limited. While the opportunity to gain informal knowledge across technologies may be available, formal movement between roles may not be possible.

5.14 NOT ALL SMALL IT DEPARTMENTS ARE IN SMBS

The normal presumption is that small IT teams are to be found in small organizations, and that is a sound and sensible rule of thumb. However, it is not always the reality. Exceptions do exist and one is worth mentioning specifically: where a larger organization exists in a very stable business context with a correspondingly stable IT environment supporting it, using very few IT staff. This situation becomes possible due to the:

- Small number of changes required since business requirements change little
- Stable (and often somewhat outdated) infrastructure – its long trend and established nature mean that failures are usually familiar in nature and easily addressed
- Concentration of IT support on a relatively small number of business-critical services.

A fairly common example of this situation was often found in local government organizations – but even here the information revolution is having a noticeable effect, with the provision of online services to the general public becoming the expectation. The required journey from stable to dynamic and innovative support service is particularly difficult for a small organization and requires considerable cultural shifts – starting with the essential need to recognize the situation and then take steps to address it.

Using the ITIL service lifecycle in small and medium-sized businesses

6

6 Using the ITIL service lifecycle in small and medium-sized businesses

Small and medium-sized businesses (SMBs) will need to draw from all five stages of the service lifecycle, and the following sections will help to determine the best potential ways to scale down without sacrificing usability or benefit.

6.1 SCALING ITIL DOWN FOR THE SMALL AND MEDIUM-SIZED BUSINESS

Most managers want to take ideas which have proved valuable elsewhere and try them out in their own environment. This is sensible practice – it is after all the philosophy upon which ITIL is based. However, no two organizations are alike, and in order to translate ideas successfully from one environment to another, processes and procedures must be adapted to fit.

While some ITIL processes scale down easily and function equally well in small or large environments, most will break if scaled down too far.

An underlying principle of this publication is to consider how scaling down affects the elements of ITIL and, where possible, to give ideas for adapting them. The questions to ask about scaling down are:

- Will the scaled approach be practical to use?
- Are the resources and capabilities available?
- Will it provide the expected value on investment (VOI)?

Scaling down the service lifecycle to fit the workload expected and the resources available is at the core of adapting generic best practices to small organizations.

6.2 SCALING YOUR SERVICE LIFECYCLE

It is important to remain aware that – however small the organization – the purpose is to manage the services provided, not merely to deliver isolated aspects of support or correction. However far service management is scaled, it must still contain all the key aspects that make up service management – rather as a car must contain the full range of basics required to deliver the service that the car offers. Scaling down means 'reducing in size', and while some simplification may be necessary to deliver service management with restricted resources, simply missing things out will not do the required job. Scaling down a group photo leaves all the original people on view; cutting some out is a different operation and destroys much of the purpose and the benefit. The service lifecycle needs to be scaled down, not cut down.

6.3 FOCUSING ON THE SERVICE

While a large and/or luxury car may have some elements that are not considered essential in all circumstances, there is a minimum set of essential features; without these components, it is not a car at all. These features effectively define the nature of the car and are clearly set by the services required of it – in this case transportation of people and luggage on normal roads. Merely supplying most of the components – for example wheels, engine, brakes and transmission – doesn't deliver the service.

This expectation of the services of a car evolves over time – increased safety features and reliability have affected what we nowadays consider the minimum package that we would refer to as a car, and the advent of green principles and ecological concerns has seen the development of high-specification but low-size/energy cars.

Similarly in IT service provision, the elements essential for it to be considered the required service will change – and what constitutes essential service is a requirement that must be understood by any service provider who wishes to be successful.

Many organizations have learnt that there is a logical approach to adapting ITIL to circumstances, which helps to justify VOI and delivers an approach that works in an SMB.

Table 6.1 Sample of defined elements within a service lifecycle

Customers	List all your customers by type (such as internal business unit), by company or by shared service use. This will make it easier to connect a customer to a service catalogue item.
Budget	Depending on the level of granularity of your financial reporting, list budgets according to customer or service.
Services	Even if you do not yet have a formal service catalogue, list the services you provide to all your customers.
Assessments	Even informal service quality or process maturity assessments can be useful to help organize a service portfolio and to identify current and desired capabilities and resources.
Resources	■ Financial capital ■ Infrastructure ■ Applications ■ People
Opportunities	Developing a list of potential IT service offerings from the business strategic plans of your customers is a good place to begin looking for opportunities. Customer and IT staff feedback, suggestions and proposals that might have been reviewed then forgotten can also give insight into future opportunities.
Projects	All IT service-related projects that are planned or under way.
Partners and suppliers	All suppliers you deal with.
Relationships	List the relationships you are a part of in the course of delivering services. Include customers, suppliers and interdepartmental relationships.
Data/information	Inventory and list the types of data and information that you currently collect. An exhaustive list is not the objective here, but determine the categories of data you have, such as customer profiles, services, configuration item information, human resource information, monitoring data, network capacity usage data, change management, assets, incidents, problems, service level agreements, contracts etc.
Processes	List the processes you currently use that include ITIL, and other processes whether from a proprietary framework or your own internal processes.
Functions	List the functions in your organization that use the processes identified above.

6.4 FINDING YOUR EXISTING SERVICE LIFECYCLE

The ITIL guidance has wide-ranging adaptability, but always needs tailoring to the specific circumstances it is applied to. That, of course, is the purpose of this publication – to help focus those adapting to a small environment.

The core of ITIL is the service lifecycle, so any organization, large or small, needs to focus initially on the services that it delivers to its customers, along with as clear as possible a picture of who those customers are.

There are elements of service provision, common to every organization, which demonstrate a pattern or lifecycle of use. Table 6.1 identifies some of these. Creating the list for a specific organization turns it into a useful tool that will highlight starting points and areas which will deliver quick gains for the organization.

6.4.1 Organizing your service lifecycle

Using the list you have created, place these into their respective place according to lifecycle phase. The list in Table 6.2 may be a useful guide.

6.5 UNDERSTANDING YOUR VALUE CREATION POTENTIAL

Once you have identified the elements you currently have or are proposing, you need to understand how these create value for your customers. This analysis can often identify services or activities you currently undertake, but which do not provide value or support business outcomes. These are prime targets for freeing extra resources (people, money etc.) to focus instead on areas that do deliver value.

This focusing of available resources onto the most productive areas is the single key factor for success in many small organizations that need to get good return from their best assets and most able people.

Once an organization has looked at its service lifecycle, improvements are often quickly visible.

The lifecycle stages are arbitrary segments of the continuum of service management. Most especially in smaller organizations, individuals are very likely to have a range of responsibilities at any given time, filling simultaneous roles across the lifecycle. Nonetheless, it is convenient to examine the impacts and the opportunities within each stage of the lifecycle for small organizations.

Table 6.2 Example list for organizing a service lifecycle

Strategy	Design	Transition	Operation	Improvement
Budgets	Architecture	Changes	Incidents	Ideas
Customers	Standards	Releases	Problems	Experiences
Services	OLAs	CIs	Events	Statistics
Assessments	Contracts	Data	Technicians	Opinions
Capabilities	Suppliers	Information	Service desk	Critics
Resources	Relationships	Knowledge	Functions	Customer feedback
Assets	Partners	Projects	Processes	Statistics
Opportunities	SLAs			

Service strategy for small and medium-sized businesses

7

7 Service strategy for small and medium-sized businesses

Strategy is exceedingly important to any small organization, because mistakes can have a faster impact than in a larger environment. The smaller scale makes it harder to establish the central importance of strategy, to stand back from everyday operations, involve stakeholders and make sound discussions on services – which to develop, which to maintain and which to retire.

The luxury of a separate, well-funded and well-informed strategy unit is unlikely, and so the tasks of strategic thinking, planning and implementation will be part-time responsibilities, often taken on by the management team in addition to operational control. This can make it hard to be objective, so be sure to self-police and try to maintain a degree of formality and documentation – trying to be sure real benefits will/do exist.

In small organizations, those creating the strategy are likely also to be involved with its delivery and be positively or negatively impacted by strategic decisions. Acceptance of the strategy is critical to maintaining a hands-on approach. Direct involvement in delivering the strategy, by those impacted in a small organization, can mean service strategy can be more directed, be more easily maintained, and kept relevant.

Minimize the bureaucracy but make sure you cover the essentials with some formality. Force yourself to ask and answer the following questions:

- Who are the stakeholders?
- What do they see as value?
- Can you measure it?
- If not, what can you do instead?

Ways of measuring usefulness are very much a strategy concern and of key importance to the SMB. Usefulness is a function of the business requirement, not of the technology's abilities. Unfortunately for many small organizations, business strategy itself is neglected and the answers are hard to find; time and resources are short and the temptation is to fall back onto judging technology by its capabilities rather than by the requirements of the business.

Regardless of size, every organization must have a service strategy. This allows the organization to see its value-producing capability needed in the future, while exploiting its current resources and capabilities. Service strategy is driven from a prime objective – achieving business outcomes.

The basic service strategy for an SMB should contain:

- The management of a service portfolio
- The ability to monitor patterns of service demand
- A model for financial management.

When customer needs are predictable, well established and well defined, the service provider can afford to look inward and focus on 'the one best way'. But customer needs often shift. Customers may encounter increased competition, financial problems or the need to improve their own internal efficiencies. When customer needs become less stable, the service provider may fall into a management trap where internal efficiency is confused with effectiveness or external efficiency. For instance, what is less effective than an engineering team that quickly turns out elegant system designs for the wrong service?

- **Internal efficiency** – the efficient use of production resources; also referred to as productivity
- **External efficiency** – the external effectiveness of the service provider as perceived by its customer; also referred to as customer-perceived quality.

7.1 BUILDING BLOCKS

Figure 7.1 shows the three main building blocks a service provider must manage in order to retain superior performance.

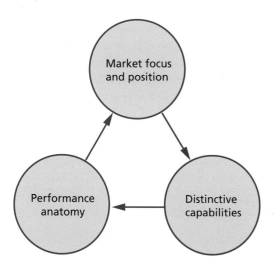

Figure 7.1 Building blocks for superior performance

7.1.1 Market focus and position
The basic requirements to manage market focus and position are:

- Build and manage valuable service portfolios

- Achieve optimal scale through sourcing strategies
- Exploit positioning advantages in the value network
- Identify and possibly offer new services
- Improve customer service
- Enter alternative market spaces.

7.1.2 Distinctive capabilities
High-performance service providers have great clarity about the resources and capabilities that contribute to facilitating customer outcomes. They understand the need to build capabilities that are demonstrably better and, in the short term, difficult to replicate by competing alternatives. This includes mastering technical capabilities and excelling at innovation, as well as lower-cost structures and customer know-how.

7.1.3 Performance anatomy
This comprises a set of organizational 'mindsets' that are measurable and actionable by organizational leadership. These mindsets drive important differences in behaviour – from individual employees to those of the service provider itself – which lead to better customer outcomes. The focus is on creating cultural and organizational characteristics that move the service provider toward its goal of outperforming competing alternatives.

7.2 THE SMB SERVICE PORTFOLIO

Understand your service portfolio first. This creates the perfect starting point that underlies how you should adapt ITIL to your circumstances.

Defining the service portfolio helps the SMB to:

■ Define required capabilities and resources
■ Develop an accurate service catalogue
■ Establish a base for building configuration information
■ Provide focus on what to measure
■ Create links to business value
■ Document and facilitate prioritization of improvement investment.

A service portfolio is the ideal way of tracking and managing investments in services that are tagged to business outcomes and therefore providing value to the business.

7.2.1 The ingredients of a service portfolio

■ **The service pipeline** An inventory of proposed services, services still in the design stage, supporting business cases and identified service improvements yet to be implemented
■ **The service catalogue** Services available for use and those in live operation. The service catalogue is divided into two parts:
  ● The technical service catalogue which contains the component level inventory of service assets, contracts and operational level agreements
  ● The business service catalogue: a customer-facing inventory of business services available and their associated service level agreements (SLAs)
■ **Retired services** Services tagged for retirement for which no further investments are viable.

It is important to establish and maintain a service portfolio. It doesn't need to be a more than a spreadsheet – but it SHOULD exist. The catalogue is important, but for small organizations the

pipeline is also vital – once this exists it facilitates early endorsement or rejection of possible future investments. Early decisions deliver the best value from available resources (small organizations rarely have the money to put into speculative ideas) and when they do, they should be deliberate and visible decisions. The list you created to identify and organize your service lifecycle can be a good starting point to begin creating the service portfolio.

As mentioned above, the elements of the service portfolio – pipeline, catalogue and retired services – do not need to be developed and maintained in complex and expensive detail to begin to pay benefits.

The service portfolio for an SMB requires the identification and documentation of possible services – initially a reflection of the customers' desires. The progress of these potential services through a defined set of life stages constitutes the portfolio. These life stages might include:

■ Discussion with customers
■ Cost/benefit considerations
■ Specification with customers and discussion with stakeholders
■ Approval/rejection by business change authority
■ Development
■ Testing and preparation.

When the service goes 'live', it moves from the pipeline into the catalogue.

None of this requires any sophisticated technology; this simple level of progress-recording can be maintained in a spreadsheet, using a simple database or with pencil and paper.

Adopting the principle of re-use and available skills, it may be relevant to discuss the requirement with any sales experts within the organization who will be very familiar with the concept of a pipeline and may be well placed to offer advice in maintaining relevant records.

7.2.2 Patterns of demand

Part of successfully managing your service portfolio, and hence your services, is to understand how customers use your services. This creates increased awareness of the patterns of demand for your services and can improve your decision-making about investing in services, capabilities and resources and managing them more efficiently.

This requires codifying the pattern of business activity (PBA) and creating user profiles (UPs) mapped to these patterns. This is powerful intelligence for predicting and managing demand. A scaled version of this is fairly simple.

1 For each of the services in your portfolio, list the main types of activity that occur in the use of the service. You will want to create a list of activities that is relevant to your own organization but as a start consider these:

- Remote access of the service
- Establishing bandwidth requirements
- Remote technical support
- Onsite technical support
- Impact by service interruption
- Variations in service usage – e.g. across day, week or year; affected by weather or other external influences
- Processed transactions
- Access via wireless mobile device.

2 Now rate each of these on a scale of high to low usage.

Table 7.1 shows an example using the above activities. The activity column indicates the base service elements used in the delivery of the messaging service. The matrix of activity levels forms the business pattern of activity. PBA10 represents a typical pattern of business activity for the messaging service. There can be many profiles, depending on user habits.

3 Do this for each service in the service portfolio.

4 Create a list of categories of users who use the service and tag each with a profile of how

Table 7.1 Example of a codified pattern of the business activity of a service

Service usage code: PBA10 Service: messaging	Activity levels High..Low				
Activity					
Remote access of the service	X				
Bandwidth requirements			X		
Remote technical support		X			
Onsite technical support				X	
Impact by service interruption	X				
Seasonal variation in service usage			X		
Processed transactions	X				
Service use via wireless mobile device	X				

Table 7.2 User profiles matched to patterns of business activity (PBA)

User profile	PBA profile for the user	PBA service usage codes
Senior executives	Highly mobile	PBA10 (the senior executives have this pattern of business activity for the messaging service)
	High service disruption impact	
	No seasonal variation	
	Wireless device service access	
	High remote technical support use	
Office staff	Non-mobile	
	Medium technical support usage	
	Seasonal variation	
	High onsite technical support	
Sales staff	Highly mobile	
	Medium service disruption impact	
	Wireless device service access	
	Medium remote technical support	
Manufacturing staff	Non-mobile	
	Low remote technical support usage	
	Low service disruption impact	
	Seasonal variation	
	Medium onsite technical support usage	

they use the service from the codified PBA (see Table 7.2).

As you complete this exercise, you begin to understand how your customers use your services and that there are variations depending on who the users are. This can help you establish core and specialized service packages, differentiate your service offerings, customize packages by need and, most importantly, establish well-known demand patterns that will drive capacity planning, investment planning and decisions for launching additional services or retiring existing services.

This is a powerful and useful part of service strategy that an SMB can employ to create a competitive advantage and maintain a healthy level of fiscal and capacity management.

7.3 FINANCIAL MANAGEMENT

Financial management for the SMB is not optional. The line between the financial success and failure of an SMB is small and the role that IT service provision plays in supporting and delivering financial management is integral. Often, the level of investment in enabling technology is comparatively high on the SMB balance sheet. Responsible financial management of these investments is critical.

The ITIL financial management process is comprehensive and involves:

- Service valuation
- Financial planning
- Investment analysis
- Accounting
- Budgeting
- Compliance with relevant regulations, industry requirements, corporate policies etc.
- Variable cost dynamics
- Service provisioning cost analysis
- Business impact analysis (BIA)
- Funding models
- Return on investment (ROI).

For an SMB, the financial management process can be adapted to scale by focusing on the critical elements that would cause unnecessary risk to the financial health of the organization if they were not in place.

The type of adaptation will vary depending on the depth of the IT investment portfolio, but basic ingredients should include:

- Service valuation: a determination of direct, indirect and shared costs for each service
- Accounting: the budget and expenditure tracking and reporting, preferably identified by service
- Financial model: the method of accruing expenditures and recovering costs

- Value on investment: projections of VOI and monitoring of these.

The mechanisms for establishing and managing these need not be complex or involve specialized tools. As a minimum, any adaptation should include a cycle of planning, monitoring, analysis and reporting, so that information is available in a format that triggers timely decisions about the VOI of services within the service portfolio.

Every business will have some existing investment in budget and expenditure management technology. IT organizations should leverage this investment and use similar or shared technology for this purpose.

7.3.1 Organizational design

Those used to working in large establishments may well take the design of their organizations for granted – something imposed from above and changed during restructures – a source of employee cynicism for over 2,000 years. While generic concepts apply to all sizes of organization, one specific element of the maintenance and update of organizational design is particularly worthy of note in the SMB context. The accepted steps in organizational design emphasize early consideration of key people – and an SMB's success often rests on the nature (and availability) of such individuals.

In large organizations, when vacancies occur the norm is to use the existing job role to form the specification for their replacement – effectively to recruit to replace. This works well in larger, traditional and relatively stable environments. In smaller organizations a different approach can often be more successful, reflecting the reality of the small-scale operation.

Within the smallest organizations, the few individuals will each have multiple roles, and many tasks will be delivered using external resources. In these circumstances it is often much more effective when vacancies arise to keep recruitment targets more general – select the most suitable person and then re-assess the allocation of roles among staff and external resources. This offers significant potential benefits:

- Easier adjustment to current requirements and circumstances, rather than sticking with existing structure
- Focusing on the critical human interaction and compatibility aspects within smaller working groups
- Making best use of available talents – for example a new person may bring capacity planning skills from a previous job, which would allow that task to become insourced while other tasks may move to external contract supply.

Service design for small and medium-sized businesses

8

8 Service design for small and medium-sized businesses

The principles of service design are applicable to organizations of any size. For the SMB, scaling will involve addressing at a high level the five aspects of service design, i.e. the design of:

- New or changed services
- Service management systems and tools
- Technology, architecture and management systems
- Process required
- Measurement methods and metrics.

Certain activities within the service design stage of the lifecycle involve the use of highly specialized skills for such things as architectural design of infrastructure and systems, capacity modelling, service continuity delivery etc. These are areas where the SMB can take advantage of industry-offered specialist skills and look toward outsourced arrangements.

This does not mean that there is no involvement of the SMB in these areas, but that these skills can often be delivered effectively as a purchased service. The SMB must still remain accountable for establishing agreements, managing suppliers and ensuring the supply chain is managed from end to end through proper contract, operational level and service level agreement management.

The SMB can actually have distinct advantages over larger organizations in this stage of the lifecycle, because they can be closer to the business customer and are able to make decisions faster and with less bureaucracy. The cornerstone of service design is understanding customer requirements and using the best possible strategy to meet expected business outcomes. Smaller organizations often have better insights into business requirements and enjoy direct trusted relationships with the customer and suppliers. This can work to the advantage of the SMB in reducing cycle times to get solid requirements agreed and understood in the supply chain and establish realistic, no-nonsense supporting agreements.

It is likely that the same individuals will have been involved in creating the service portfolio and analysing demand patterns, so the continuity of knowledge is brought directly into the service design stage, along with ability to influence and create the needed relationships to deliver a service design package that will meet business outcomes.

Service design also deals with the design of measurement systems and processes to support services. Here the SMB also maintains an advantage in influencing the scaling of processes that are the correct size to meet the desired outcomes.

Service design for the SMB should endeavour to include not only all the main processes in this stage of the lifecycle, but also look to use industry-available managed services for specialists. The managed service industry has become a widely available commodity and costs are extremely competitive. This should not lull the SMB into automatically assuming a positive VOI. It is important to analyse this first, but it is likely that cost-effective and appropriately sized external service provision is available.

Table 8.1 Example of the service design process and activity management sourcing

SD process or activity	Possible sourcing option
Service catalogue management	**Internal:** Maintain a simple service catalogue that is generated from the service portfolio. Many standard and simple templates are available for use – both commercially and freely. See Appendix A for an example.
Service level management	**Internal:** Never outsource this type of relationship with your business customer. Use readily available templates and customize them against what you can measure and manage. See Appendix B for examples of an SLA and OLA.
Capacity management	**External:** This can be outsourced, except for PBA analysis, which should be done internally and on a regular basis. The trended results can be fed to a managed service provider for planning and costing. It makes sense to be aware of the inherent conflict in motives when assessing the need for further capacity and supplying that capacity – in spite of the extra supplier management issue, SMBs should consider separating these services.
Availability management (AM)	**External:** Activities that contribute to availability such as incident, event and monitoring can be externally sourced if cost is justifiable, but the accountability for managing the customer should remain an internal function and tied in as part of the service level management (SLM) process. The proactive activities of availability management – risk assessment, planning and design – should be considered for internal delivery, possibly with contracted expertise.
IT service continuity management	**External:** The extent of outsourcing will depend largely upon how services are managed. If many of the critical business services are managed externally, there will be a need for some central coordination of plans, analysis and development of continuity arrangements. The ITSCM initiation phase can be outsourced; indeed each stage of ITSCM from initiation to ongoing operation can benefit from external management. However, the internal IT organization must be ultimately accountable and should be active in developing the business continuity strategy and plans in collaboration with the business, to ensure proper alignment with any outsourced elements of ITSCM.
Information security management (ISM)	**Internal/external:** The policy and planning should be an internal function supplemented by external specialists if needed. The ongoing execution can be an externally procured service.
Requirements engineering	**Internal/external:** Technical architecture of infrastructure and applications can be outsourced, but involvement of internal IT and customer stakeholders should be managed internally.
Data and information management	**Internal or external:** Hosting, storage and maintenance can be an outsourced service, but policies should be developed and managed internally.
Application management	**External:** The activities around application management can safely be outsourced. This can be a cost-effective way to maintain highly specialized application management skills without providing internal staffing. However, it is important that the accountability for managing the chosen supplier(s) remains an internal function of supplier management.
Technology architecture design	**External:** The policies and requirements etc. should be fed to the external provider. This is a highly specialized function and, typically, SMBs won't have the expertise in house. Depending on the sector/nature of the business, a reliable and secure infrastructure can make or break an organization. Depending on the budgets allotted, outsourcing can greatly improve an organization's bottom line by utilizing external expertise in designing an innovative and efficient architecture. This maximizes capabilities whilst managing cost.
Process and measurement systems design	**Internal:** The execution of this activity should be kept internal. However, it is likely that acquiring external expertise in initially setting it up can greatly improve the end result. External expertise in this regard should not be used to lead or make decisions: external knowledge should be used as guidance only.
Business impact analysis (BIA)	**Internal:** SMBs have an advantage in that shared roles contain widespread knowledge within the organization among a small group of resources. This knowledge can be utilized efficiently for business impact analysis without the bureaucracy of many stakeholder views that often accompany a large organization.

8.1 BUILDING SERVICE DESIGN CAPABILITY – BUILD OR BUY?

It is important that customer and supplier relationships are managed internally and that both are involved in the service design. SMBs should seek to amalgamate external service into a few key suppliers wherever possible. Managing numerous external suppliers and their contracts can cripple a small organization. This also exposes an SMB to additional risk with multiple points of potential failure in the supply chain, as a result of neglected or improperly managed relationships, and creates high overheads in the alignment of all suppliers to achieve seamless service delivery. The over-reliance on one supplier also comes with some risk, so the SMB must seek the right balance to minimize risk, but still leverage a management supply chain.

Table 8.1 offers some guidance on a starting point for considering what to manage internally and what to consider sourcing externally.

Service transition for small and medium-sized businesses

9 Service transition for small and medium-sized businesses

Service transition is an area that can seem less difficult in many small organizations, with fewer of the complicated structures and situations that make it such a frequent cause of concern in larger organizations. Specifically, many of the causes of complication are not so common in SMBs, for example:

- Widely dispersed infrastructure
- Large training commitments – users and support
- Complex budgetary and planning requirements
- Internal politics.

However, SMBs are more likely to suffer from:

- Time and money pressures to deliver services into live operation
- Lack of resources to do relevant testing, in particular:
  - Internal resources and customer/stakeholder input to meaningful acceptance testing
  - Testing resources to trial services under transition in an environment matched to live.

Service transition will always remain a crucial area and cannot be neglected. Even in the smallest of organizations, the easiest and most common way to create incidents is through rushed, unapproved and uncontrolled changes, so neglect of service transition will cost the SMB in the longer term.

Several crucial processes associated with service transition are genuinely whole lifecycle processes, although with their main focus in service transition (service asset and configuration management, change management and knowledge management). In a small organization, with less functional or organizational division between operational teams, it should be easier to treat these processes with a single, broad focus across the whole life of a service. A key to achieving this successfully is involving all affected staff in the specification, development and improvement of the processes.

Crucially this will assist an SMB to:

- Reduce the overall costs and diminish duplication of data capture
- Encourage a single view of service management, rather than a view of process silos or lifecycle stages
- Allow synergies with related processes, tools and techniques used by equivalent processes in other parts of the organization – such as enterprise assets, organization-wide document and knowledge management and business change processes.

Ideally, the following processes should be considered critical to service transition practice:

- Service asset and configuration management
- Change management
- Release and deployment management
- Service validation and testing
- Knowledge management.

9.1 SERVICE ASSET AND CONFIGURATION MANAGEMENT

Many organizations make the fatal mistake of thinking that service asset and configuration management (SACM) is a repository of data in a tool. Say the word 'database' and most are off and running to populate the configuration management system (CMS) with every possible piece of data that technology can collect.

Service asset and configuration management is a process within ITIL that is supported by data. SACM creates a foundation for many other ITIL processes in all stages of the service lifecycle by connecting technical component information to the services it enables.

For the SMB, SACM is vitally important, but it doesn't need to be a complex process requiring expensive tools to be effective.

It is important for all organizations that they map their configuration management approach and solutions to their requirements – there is a temptation to believe that the more spent on software tools and data collection the better, but this is not the case.

9.1.1 SACM policies

As a starting point, SMBs should develop policies that establish the parameters of scope for SACM in the organization. At a minimum the following areas should be addressed:

- **Scope** Ensure that the SACM process and underlying technology are integrated with change management and release and deployment management

- **Ownership** Use a RACI matrix (Responsible–Accountable–Consulted–Informed) to define who in the organization owns, uses and is mandated to use SACM
- **Information** Define the level of detail that is beneficial for SACM information. Consider who will use the information in addition to who will maintain it.

Defining SACM policies first will help the organization to understand the purpose, goals and objectives and provide a good basis for deciding the scale of process and technology that will be needed. An unfortunate, but common, mistake made by many organizations is to skip this step and go directly into acquiring complex technology to address a simple solution.

9.1.2 SACM process

Once the initial planning is complete, the basic cycle in the SACM process lifecycle is as shown in Table 9.1.

Every SMB will have differing needs and, thus, different answers to the above questions. Keep the classification of service assets and configuration items simple, descriptive and as few in number as possible. This allows for less complex tools to support CMS information, and for retrieval and use by incident, change and release management users.

Table 9.1 A cycle in the SACM process

Identification	Control	Status accounting and reporting	Verification and audit
What information will be needed?	How will it be kept accurate?	Who must know what about assets and configuration items (CIs) at various points in time?	How will we validate accuracy of information and how often should we do so?
		How do we account for changes to the CIs?	

For a very small organization, adequate configuration management technology may be a well-maintained spreadsheet. The major benefits of SACM are driven by the relationships between configuration items and service assets that are grouped and mapped to services.

For smaller organizations, IT asset and configuration management can realistically be seen as a part of the broader asset management requirement. Certainly it would be common and good practice to incorporate assets such as telephone and networked equipment within a single approach. It may well be possible in a simple situation to consider the implementation of a configuration management system using existing data across the organization, although some modifications to deliver consistency and connectability are usually necessary.

9.2 CHANGE MANAGEMENT

SMBs have an opportunity in terms of change management to integrate the procedures for managing change across the whole organization. But again, it is essential with change, as with SACM, to introduce only the degree of complexity and control that is necessary and justified. Even in the largest organizations, attempts to force every change through detailed central change management approval are rarely successful and never cheap. SMBs should focus on pragmatism. In practice this means restricting the full force of expensive change assessment and management to those potential changes where risk/benefit has to be assessed. This really rests upon using the two simple tenets that underpin efficient (as opposed to economical or effective) change management – appropriate authorization levels (as in Figure 9.1)

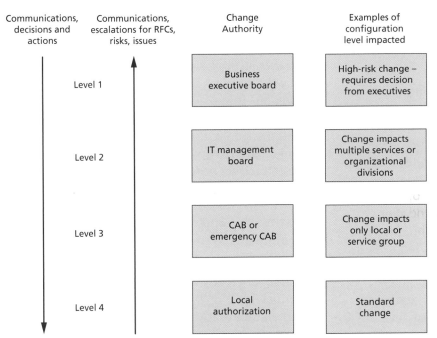

Communications, decisions and actions	Communications, escalations for RFCs, risks, issues	Change Authority	Examples of configuration level impacted
Level 1		Business executive board	High-risk change – requires decision from executives
Level 2		IT management board	Change impacts multiple services or organizational divisions
Level 3		CAB or emergency CAB	Change impacts only local or service group
Level 4		Local authorization	Standard change

Figure 9.1 Example levels of change authorization

and the use of standard changes – effectively, pre-authorization of anticipated changes.

9.2.1 Change control

Experience shows that the smaller an organization, the easier it can be to circumvent change procedures – the practical approach is to:

- Delegate authority to the lowest level consistent with business risk
- Maximize the range and applicability of standard changes
- Ensure top priority is given to full awareness of change management.

Every organization should consider a list of qualifying questions that drive decisions for whatever level of involvement in change management authorization is needed. Consider the following examples and build upon them as relevant to your organization:

- **Does this change require special funding approval?** Changes that are funded for a specific purpose will very often have a high-risk, high-impact profile. While this may not always be the case, it is often a good question to consider when profiling changes for risk and impact. The higher the two are, the greater level of visibility and authorization may be needed
- **Is this change part of regular ongoing maintenance?** Changes that are repetitive and are done as a matter of course for operational need can often be pre-approved and then carried out as standard changes. This does not necessarily mean that they are not high risk in nature, but that they have been thoroughly tested, assessed for risk and impact, and planned during regular change windows and can therefore be excluded from high levels of authorization for every change

- **Are multiple business areas affected by this change?** When one business area requests a change, it can be mistakenly considered to have a level of impact that is isolated to that business area. This is very often not the case. A positive response to this question should trigger a check that impact assessment has been properly done and that all business areas impacted have been involved in authorizing or notified prior to a change
- **If this change fails, what is the risk to critical business processes?** Even the seemingly smallest, low-risk changes can wreak havoc on business operations when they fail. Every change should have a back-out plan and be impacted to identify the critical business processes affected should the worst case occur. The higher the propensity for failure, the higher the level of visibility and authorization that may be warranted for such a change
- **Do business operations need to be halted during this change?** This type of change will likely pose a high risk to the business and so a higher level of authorization to accept the risk is warranted
- **Will our suppliers be affected by this change?** Even though a change is directed at internally managed services, external suppliers managing part of the service, or seemingly unrelated services, may be impacted by the change. While suppliers may not be 'approvers' for these types of changes in every case, prior notification and request for impact assessment may be a wise route.

You will undoubtedly have more questions like this, that when answered, will help to clarify the true impact of the change, and the level of authorization that should accompany the process of implementing it.

All those involved in and able to make changes must believe that it is beneficial for themselves and the organization as a whole to follow the change procedure. In smaller – and possibly less formal – organizations this usually means staff understanding the need and benefits rather than threats of punishment for non-compliance.

An organization is a living, integrated and dynamic structure, and changes in any part will inevitably have consequences in other areas – so the higher the level of change impact that can be understood and implemented, the more likely it is that more of the risks and benefits will have been considered. When change management focuses on technical

delivery changes, it becomes all but impossible to see consequential business benefit.

Concentrate resources on the changes that matter – change management should not be onerous and bureaucratic but should initially focus on the areas where control will bring the greatest benefit either in mitigating risk or expediting change for business advantage. Examine standard, low-risk changes and consider a simplified workflow for these.

Figure 9.2 illustrates an example of a scaled change management process.

If we overlay a scaled process on top of the full change management process (Figure 9.3), you can

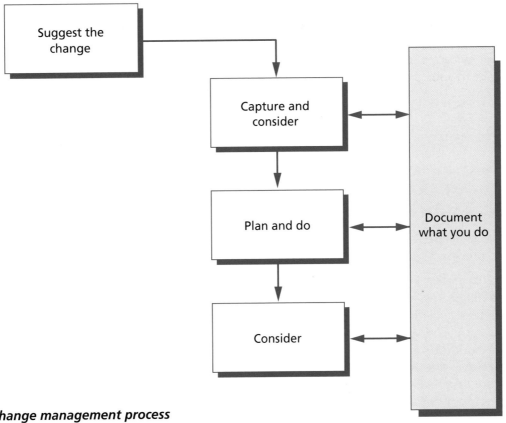

Figure 9.2 Scaled change management process

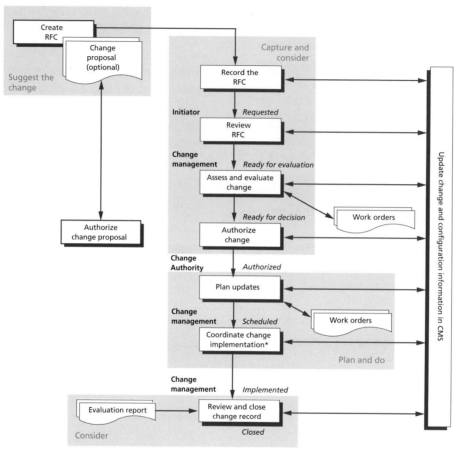

Figure 9.3 Scaled change management process overlaid on full change management process

see the main areas that would form part of the scaled process.

Scaling processes involves a review of each activity in the full process and seeking opportunities to combine activities and roles and simplify the workflow. Each SMB may have a slightly different scaled workflow depending on how it is structured, what is externally managed and how roles are assigned. It is important that a scaled process is not simply one with steps eliminated.

It is possible to successfully scale workflow by eliminating some activities, but this should not be done unless it has been carefully considered and will not compromise the overall logic, benefit and usability.

9.3 RELEASE AND DEPLOYMENT MANAGEMENT

Even though an SMB may use external managed services that may include infrastructure,

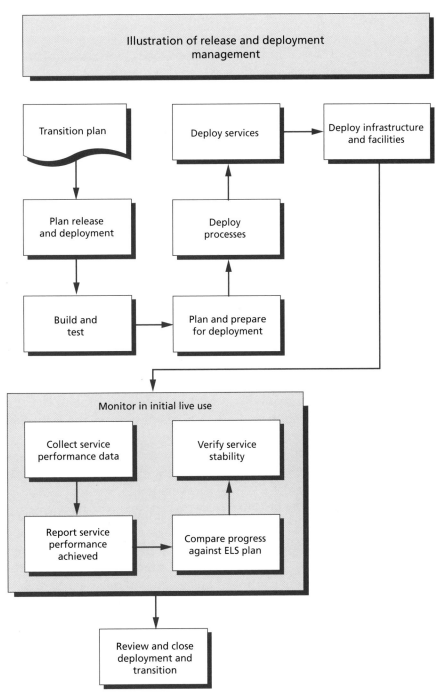

Figure 9.4 Illustration of release and deployment management

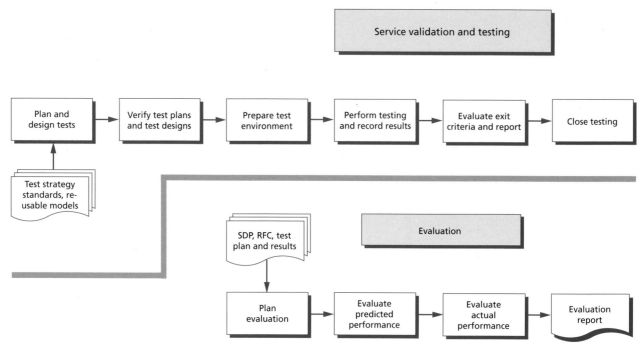

Figure 9.5 Illustration of service validation and testing and evaluation

applications, network and support, there is still the need to have policies, a process and procedures in place for releases. An SMB should ensure that these are known, accepted and integrated within supplier arrangements. Where internal release and deployment management exists, the SMB should include at a minimum the following process elements:

■ Release policies – to control how, when and who will carry out releases

■ Release plans – for larger releases where control and communication are needed

■ Service test plans – to ensure validation of expected performance of service assets

■ Deployment planning and preparation – this forms part of the release and is the opportunity to prepare the organization's stakeholders and IT teams who will be involved in deployment activities

■ Early life support (ELS) – to ensure customer needs related to the initial release phase are managed.

IT project initiatives in SMBs must be brought into the release and deployment management processes at the outset to ensure that there is control, accountability and proper management of build, test and release activities.

Even in cases where services are designed, built and tested through external suppliers, their eventual release will impact the customer. SMBs should ensure that a firm process is in place for release and deployment management to have internal

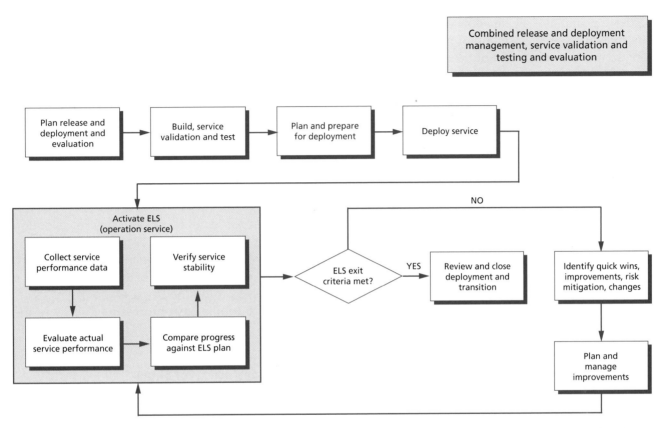

Figure 9.6 Combined process for release and deployment, service validation and testing and evaluation

involvement at various stages of the development of the service.

Figures 9.4 to 9.6 are illustrations of full-scale process flows for release and deployment management, service validation and testing, and evaluation.

For an average SMB, the above two process illustrations could place a heavy burden on the resources trying to execute these as part of release and deployment. Figure 9.6 shows a scaled-down version which combines all three processes into a manageable size.

9.3.1 Service validation and testing

In larger organizations and large-scale development, service validation and testing can be a complex process involving many stakeholders and resources throughout the service transition lifecycle. SMBs can scale this process by integrating it with release and deployment build and test activities, making sure that acceptance criteria and quality assurance (QA) criteria are met.

Effective testing is greatly supported by the availability of a relevant test environment. The ultimate is a separate environment which accurately simulates all elements of the live environment, in which testing of new and changed services can take place without compromising the live services. However, only the largest, richest and/or most safety-critical situations can hope to have a full, exact and separate test environment. For most SMBs only a limited test environment will be possible.

However, SMBs, like all organizations, should consider how to deliver the best value of testing for the money available.

Elements to consider in planning and maintaining a test environment include:

■ Base justification for testing on the damage caused by previously undetected errors, which would have been detected by improvements to the test environment. Previous failures are likely to indicate where the best initial return would lie

■ Running testing within the live environment during live operation should be avoided whenever possible – the initial aim of testing is to create failure situations, and these often cause disruption across a whole environment. However, a portable test environment that can be loaded during non-operational times can be a successful strategy

■ Establishing reusable test environments and data can be very cost-effective, but does require initial cost and business justification.

One of the benefits of combining service validation and testing with release and deployment in a smaller organization is that validation can be used to help structure the release and deployment process flow by using the key checkpoints in validation to form a basic process step.

Table 9.2 Example of basic structure for reviewing information index needs for SKMS

Type of information	User groups who may need it	What it might be needed for
Events	Service desk	User login errors or password resets
	Incident management	Infrastructure issues or threshold information
	Problem management	Actionable events for preventing incidents
	Change management	Trending and analysis
	Demand management	Demand forecasts and planning
Known errors	Service desk	Incident triage
	Business users	User self-help
	Release and deployment management	Trending and analysis for future releases
	Application management	Generating and reviewing for infrastructure and application management
	Infrastructure management	
	Problem management	
Service requests	Service desk	Trending and analysis for service portfolio pipeline
	Business managers	
	Change management	Business decisions on service needs and demand
	Business users	Self-help logging and tracking

9.4 KNOWLEDGE MANAGEMENT

Knowledge management is essential for SMBs because of the combined roles and responsibilities that often exist, the need to share specialized knowledge and maximize the information captured through the various lifecycle processes, and the cost savings that can be realized by managing information efficiently and avoiding duplication. The use of a well-structured service knowledge management system (SKMS) can ensure that everyone in the SMB can make use of information regardless of where it originates. The SKMS does not need to be a sophisticated, complex system, in fact templates and spreadsheets could suffice for a very small SKMS, but the critical part of connecting information and understanding how it can and will be best used is what gives the SKMS its value.

Think of the SKMS as a reference library, where all the information that the IT organization generates is catalogued so that no matter who you are or where you work in the organization, you can search for information and gain use and decision capability that is relevant and useful to you.

For an SMB, a simple index system can be the start of your SKMS. Using a few meaningful categories of information, either by IT department, process or function, and then listing or linking searchable records can direct users of the index to the source information. This alleviates the need to build a sophisticated system. Spend time planning what types of information will be useful and by whom, so the indexing can be as intuitive as possible. As your use of SKMS information grows, so will your appetite for more a formalized SKMS system, as will your understanding of your needs.

Table 9.2 shows a few basic types of information matched to users to build upon. Use this as a structure for examining the various types of information you have and how it might be useful to index or build into your SKMS. This list is not meant to be all-inclusive, but to help you structure a review and build upon it.

Service operation for small and medium-sized businesses

10

10 Service operation for small and medium-sized businesses

Service operation is often where the majority of the IT budget is spent. It therefore makes good sense that this area is a prime focus for the establishment and improvement of service management practices – a good degree of depth and control is sensible and likely to repay investment quickly. Much of the information generated during the management of services will be produced during the service operation phase of the lifecycle, and the value of this information to all other parts of the service lifecycle is enormous.

Even in highly outsourced SMB environments, the primary accountability for service value to the customer rests internally within the IT organization.

The key scaled processes and functions that should always exist are:

- Event management
- Incident management
- Problem management
- Monitoring and control
- Access management
- IT operations management
- Security management
- Request fulfilment
- Service desk.

These processes and functions can be outsourced or managed internally depending on what is justifiable, but the SMB should always control the policy and process acceptance of these with external suppliers.

There is a great opportunity to combine roles, activities and processes in this part of the service lifecycle to help scale and adapt them to the SMB. Incident, request and problem processes can be scaled into a hybrid process, but be sure that problem management does not become an extension of managing incidents. A clear hand-off from incident to problem should exist so that service availability is not compromised by trying to determine root cause or becoming focused on solving the problem at the expense of restoring service to the customer.

The daily activities within IT operations, monitoring and control, event management, security and access management can be streamlined into a single set of process activities to help ensure they are usable and manageable to the SMB.

The use of customer self-help technology can provide benefit to the SMB by reducing workload at the service desk. For example, customers can search the SKMS for answers to questions about the use of applications and search for workarounds to known errors. A self-help request management interface to the incident and/or request management systems can take advantage of creating incident and request records, automated routeing of incidents and requests, saving time and calls to the service desk.

With limited resources it makes sense to describe service operations procedures to monitor the operational delivery and respond as required to user needs and issues.

Many of the elements are very much routine, requiring ongoing process elements that react to business as usual outputs, and collect data against possible future analysis needs – i.e. they do not trigger direct user-related actions. The more limited the available resources are, the more relevant it becomes to prioritize the collection of routine data – establishing and then focusing on the data that is more relevant and useful to the organization. Factors that will affect an SMB's choice in this respect might include:

- Legal or industry requirements
- Analysis – or less formal indications from service desk staff and users – of previous pain points and where information either has been useful in the past or its absence was noted as causing delays
- Ease of capture
- Independence of data – if the data is intended primarily to detect trends, usage levels etc., then do not collect different data elements that show the same or similar trends; instead, identify the cheapest and easiest, and extrapolate the others if they are required.

Other elements require consequential actions – incidents are the major example, but active responses are also required to other tasks such as access permissions and service requests.

Of course, many of these tasks will be delivered via third parties, and while any element can be outsourced, however small the organization, monitoring and owning of the user and customer interface are essential if good service is to be established and maintained. Where shared resources are a part of the service delivery mechanism, event and incident management are likely to be wrapped up as part of the overall service. This trend is likely to increase in the future as industry moves towards managed cloud computing, web-hosted facilities and software as a service. Where small organizations have an affiliation to a larger organization that can coordinate services – and small government organizations are the most common example of this worldwide – ensuring that relevant information is delivered in the best format is certainly worthwhile.

10.1 REQUEST FULFILMENT

Within many organizations, request fulfilment is treated as part of the incident management process. While this can be an effective way to handle requests, often they are simply considered within the incident prioritization and given the lowest level of response. This can lead to an unnecessarily low perception of overall service quality. Requests fall outside of the definition of an incident and are not tied to service disruption. They will often need to be integrated with other areas of service management such as change management, facilities management and IT operations management. The historical grouping of requests as part of an incident has been driven by the notion of ensuring a single point of contact (SPOC) for the customer to interface with IT service provision. Using a SPOC today does not necessarily need to be a call to the service desk. The use of customer self-help, in the form of a web-based request system, an e-mail form or telephony solution, can offer a more mature routeing of requests without burdening the service desk staff with incidents.

The SMB should give careful consideration to the SLA commitments for requests and promote them with the customer as part of responsive, customer-centric service practices.

10.2 INCIDENT MANAGEMENT

In the IT organization of an SMB, incident management is likely to comprise the core of everyday responsibility in addressing users' issues. Successful discharge of communication and responsibility requires an understanding of how the needs of the user will vary from those of the customer – and of course that in turn rests on an understanding of those two important – but separate – roles.

Customers are the reason the service exists, and they deal with the required utilities and warranties that will be delivered. Effectively, therefore, the customer has a financial role – being crucial to decisions as to what can be afforded and justified. This may be direct (as in paying for the service from their budget) or indirect (as in being responsible for producing the business case that justifies a service). For example, the chief financial officer (CFO) would be considered the customer for an invoicing service.

Users – as the name implies – are those who actually use the service – typically making use of it to deliver their work commitments. A simple example is finance staff using the invoicing service to create invoices. While they might have been consulted and asked for an opinion, they will not have made decisions about the nature of the service. Their focus when contacting the service desk is likely to be 'How can I get on with doing my job?' rather than concerns with long-term service costs or characteristics.

The roles of customer and user are exactly that – roles – and the same person may fill both roles at different times. While the personnel manager may take objective and difficult cost-based decisions about the need to opt for 9–5 rather than 24/7 support for the HR system, when they have access issues they will be seeking quick restoration, not considering the relevance of previous value judgements.

In situations where resources are scarce, there is a tendency to have informal information management in place, and this can exacerbate an already overloaded work effort. The capture, tracking and use of incident information should take a high priority in the SMB, since it will provide more effective and efficient use of staff time and ability to respond and restore services to the customer. Even with a village culture and the tendency for informal support contact, formal process management should be embedded to ensure that opportunities for monitoring events and incidents, and for analysing incident information, are not lost to casual support activities.

Where there is a wide diversity of users, either geographically or of expertise, it makes sense to identify local systems administrators (LSAs), or super users, from user staff. Selecting LSAs:

- Lightens the load for the ITSM service desk
- Provides users with someone familiar with their working environment as a first point of contact
- Filters out trivial and multiple incidents.

In order to keep an accurate picture of customer concerns and incidents, LSAs should log all the incidents they receive and resolve. This will be more feasible if they have access to the software support tool on which incidents are logged.

While accepted best practice dictates universal capture of every incident, the pragmatic reality is that no organization captures every incident; some are resolved by users without any logging being possible, some are dealt with locally and some may be missed through pressure and volume in times of major outages. The benefits of capturing absolutely everything should not be allowed to outweigh the overheads, especially in the kind of organization where pragmatism and informality are required for survival. There are tangible benefits to local resolution of incidents, whether by formally recognized super users, local administrators etc. or by informal local expertise. Where resources are limited and/or distributed across different groups with different approaches and constraints, the first focus is to capture and address incidents that need central attention.

Moving on – with developing maturity – to capture locally resolved incidents is worthwhile in terms of identifying and removing repeating incidents and underlying causes, and should be planned for and introduced.

Figure 10.1 illustrates a scaled incident management process and the key activities that should be included.

Let's overlay the above scaled process with the full incident management process (see Figure 10.2) to illustrate how activities have been scaled down into a simplified process.

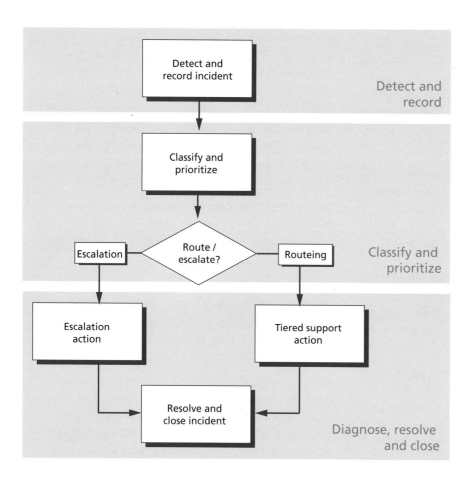

Figure 10.1 Scaled incident management process

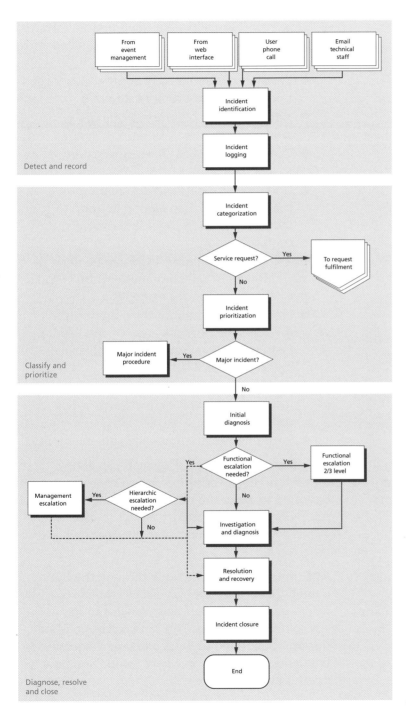

Figure 10.2 Full incident management process

10.2.1 Service desk codes of conduct

Service desks see themselves as the single point of contact between customers and IT services; however, business managers and customers see them as the contact point for the whole of the IT organization. In order to fulfil that role, service desks must adopt a code of conduct which specifies:

- Never blaming other parts of the IT organization for any problems
- Accepting comments, suggestions and complaints about any aspect of the IT directorate's service, logging them, and channelling them to the right person
- Having enough knowledge to understand such calls, or making sure that the customer is contacted by someone else who does.

10.2.2 Coping with a part-time service desk role

In an SMB, it will probably not be possible to justify staffing the service desk full time. What often happens is that the people responsible for taking service desk calls work on other things as well. However, they are then constantly interrupted – the very thing the service desk system was designed to avoid. Look at the potential for widening the service desk's coverage to provide a business service. Techniques that may help include:

- Medical treatment concept – full service desk services are available at set times – that is, office hours; frequently asked questions (FAQs) and emergency contact information are available for the rest of the working day. This at least reduces the level of interruption to IT staff, but it does rely on having understanding customers

- Where staff are allocated full-time to a service desk role – then troughs of work are filled with proactive tasks – this might involve:
  - Carrying out audits of IT or other assets via telephone calls or remote software
  - Notifying users of any new changes or workarounds
  - Contacting users to check satisfaction or just to keep in touch
  - Updating manuals and documentation – the service desk is in a good position to judge users' levels of understanding and comprehension
- Introducing automation – this can be done by using intelligent telephone systems that would give callers options, for example:
  - Press 2 for news about the current situation (perhaps the network is down and will be restored in 30 minutes, which will explain many users' problems)
  - Press 9 to record a message logging your incident which will be dealt with in due course
  - Press 0 to talk to someone in an emergency.

Over-use of automatic call systems can annoy rather than help – ensure any such system is designed to make the caller's experience better, e.g. by saving time – and try always to offer a simple route to someone in an emergency or urgent need.

Additionally, this can be done through the use of web-based technology, via an intranet site where users can get self-help answers to some less complex problems. This can be accomplished through publishing of FAQs and user guides and then educating users on where to find and how to use this knowledge.

10.2.3 Matching service desk processes to need

Procedures should be no more complicated than they need to be and should reflect customers' perceptions of incidents, rather than those of the IT. For example, a complex structure of incident classification is neither necessary nor helpful. More intuitive is using three levels of priority, an approach proven over thousands of years in situations such as categorizing the wounded (triage).

How incidents are ranked must reflect their impact upon the business they support, and not ITSM criteria. For example, a broken printer is just a routine incident to IT. However, to the business it could be very serious if important month-end printing was taking place. To make ranking criteria clear, everyday language should be used to describe the priority levels, for example:

- **Priority level 1** I can't do something important
- **Priority level 2** Please fix as soon as you can, but I can get on with something else for now
- **Priority level 3** I can live without it for a while.

Organizations increasing their ITSM maturity may choose to have more than three incident categories if they observe that only having three is leading to 'level 2' being used for the vast majority of incidents – where there is a 'middle' level, it can be used no matter what, rather than really trying to determine the actual impact. Alternatively, an awareness campaign to recognize the value of using the full range and categorizing properly may be successful in changing behaviour.

10.3 PROBLEM MANAGEMENT

Many organizations choose to pay little attention to formal problem management without realizing that this is an area that can vastly improve service quality. In an SMB, making problem management a priority can not only improve service quality, but reduce the costly expense of dealing with recurring incidents. A prerequisite for even a scaled-down version of problem management is having good, consistently classified, incident data from which to detect patterns of recurrence. If resources do not exist to appoint a problem manager, then an incident manager or technical analyst can play a part-time role in analysing incident data, identifying problems and root causes.

There is genuine danger in not separating incident and problem processes, including:

- A focus solely on restoration that almost encourages the retention of underlying problems that create easy-to-solve incidents
- An inability to resist investigation of underlying causes when a simple restoration of service is what is needed.

However, although the roles need to be separated, this can work successfully even when those roles are combined within an individual or team. The crucial element is retaining the correct focus at the correct moment. Lessons from everyday life can help – we all understand the need, when faced with a flooded kitchen, to turn off the water and dry the floor; but we then move on to tracking down the cause of the leak and preventing its recurrence without the need necessarily for more than one person to be involved.

10.4 EVENT MANAGEMENT

As the process responsible for monitoring the infrastructure, event management (EM) offers the SMB a prime opportunity to make use of automation to help manage the reliability of services and streamline workflow into proactive and reactive functions. This is also an area within service management where there are many external suppliers offering competitive, comprehensive event management services. The SMB should consider establishing event management policies for processes that will be monitored, the types of events in the organization that will be categorized and the workflow associated with each category. A scaled event management process must include the basic activities of:

- Detecting
- Filtering
- Correlating
- Triggering
- Alerts
- Routeing.

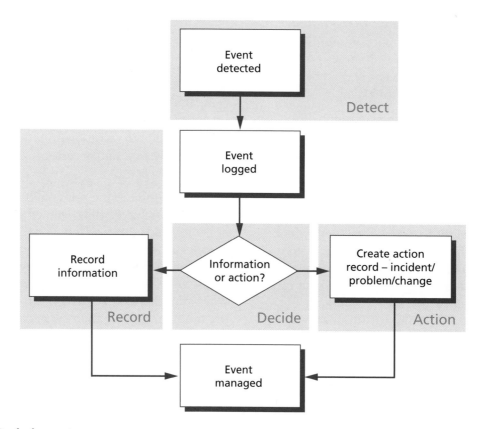

Figure 10.3 Scaled event management process

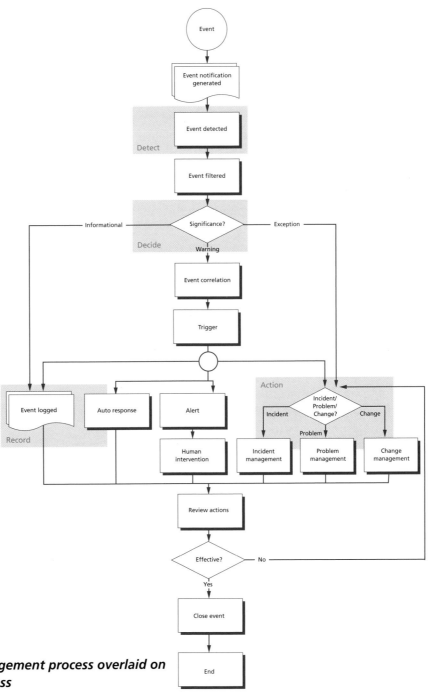

Figure 10.4 Scaled event management process overlaid on a full event management process

Information from events will flow into many other process areas such as incident, problem, service asset and configuration and knowledge management. The SMB must ensure that responses from filtered events are streamlined into these other scaled processes in a logical, workable way. Look for further opportunities to automate these downstream process activities by utilizing event information. Examples of this are:

■ Automatically populating incident, problem, change or configuration records with details from event records that are pertinent to the response needed

■ Providing information to the knowledge data repository about behavioural parameters of the infrastructure

■ Trend reports for downstream processes for further improvement opportunities.

10.4.1 Event management within incident management

Even though a small organization may not use a formal process, event management will often casually form part of the incident management process.

Event monitoring can provide valuable insights into the behaviour of the IT environment before an incident reaches a point where it causes service disruption. For this reason, it is wise to scale the event management process into a quick formalized method for detecting, recording and deciding if action is needed. Figure 10.3 shows a scaled view of the main elements of event management.

Figure 10.4 shows how the scaled event management process looks when overlaid on top of the full EM process. This helps to see which are the important activities in the process flow that must be kept as part of a scaled version of the EM process.

Continual service improvement for small and medium-sized businesses

11

11 Continual service improvement for small and medium-sized businesses

In many organizations, continual service improvement (CSI) is still an abstract concept. Improvement opportunities are serendipitously uncovered and most improvements are driven by the consequences of service failures, or unhappy customers.

A growing awareness of the importance of formal CSI practices is becoming embedded in organizations. Cost management, competitive advantage and focusing the organization on a service mindset are all potential benefits of CSI.

The community atmosphere of the SMB offers distinct advantages for formalizing CSI. Closeness to the customer may offer greater opportunities to have more insight into business objectives, how they change and how IT can improve to support them.

Central to CSI are three processes:

- Seven-step improvement
- Service measurement
- Service reporting.

Each of these processes is important for the SMB. Every organization needs to measure and report on services in order to identify and justify improvements. The seven-step improvement process fits any size of organization. The key for the SMB is realizing what should be measured and having the resources to do this.

The seven-step improvement process

The seven-step improvement process spans not only the management organization but the entire service lifecycle. It is a cornerstone of continual service improvement, and the steps can be summarized as follows:

1 Define what you should measure
2 Define what you can measure
3 Gather the data
4 Process the data
5 Analyse the data
6 Present and use the information
7 Implement corrective action.

The knowledge gained from this process is used to optimize, improve and correct services. Managers identify issues and present solutions. The corrective actions that need to be taken to improve the service are communicated and explained to the organization. Following this step the organization establishes a new baseline and the cycle begins anew.

For more information on the seven-step improvement process, see the core publication, *Continual Service Improvement* (TSO, 2007).

The three CSI processes are closely linked. Making improvements without being able to measure them will not help you to determine if they are having the intended effect. Without reporting, measurements become best guesses, are not reliable and cannot be used as convincing evidence in support of additional resources to drive improvements through the lifecycle.

If you are embarking on CSI for the first time, use the seven-step improvement process first to determine what you have the capability to measure and report on. Then use service measurement and service reporting to drive measurable, justifiable service improvements.

As part of ongoing service management, you will collect a variety of information. From incident records, changes, configuration items, capacity, monitoring, knowledge, surveys etc. a wealth of wisdom can be derived. By following the seven-step process, you will determine what types of information you have, what you need to know, what decisions will be made with the information, and then how best to analyse and use it.

Determining what to measure is one of the most important steps. Millions of dollars are wasted each year by organizations which collect and maintain information that is never used or is not accurate. Neither of these is acceptable.

For the SMB, wise choices in what needs to be measured and what can be measured are not only critical to good service management, but can be the first place to apply improvement.

What to measure will depend upon what business outcomes are being supported and what information sources are available. A basic measurement tenet for the SMB is the simpler the information, the more reliable it will be.

Make sure that service reporting meets the objective of whatever decisions it will support, who needs to see it and how. Most technology today offers a multitude of reporting functionality.

However, try not to be enticed by the volume, as opposed to the content, of the reports that you can produce. Focus on the following priorities when considering CSI:

1 Using your service portfolio and discussions with your customers, list what knowledge about service performance is important. If the list is too large, try to prioritize it by 'must have', 'should have' and 'nice to have'.

2 Use the list of information types that you identified in your service strategy stage when organizing your service lifecycle. That tells you what you currently have to work from.

3 Compare the two lists and determine if there are gaps in what you must measure and what you can measure. Hint – here is the first improvement opportunity!

4 Define how you will gather the information, and who needs to be involved. A RACI matrix (used for defining roles and responsibilities) may be helpful for this.

5 Define how the information must be analysed to meet the first objective above.

6 Define the outputs, target audiences and frequency of the reports.

7 Start doing it.

If you discover that some of your data may not be reliable or current, don't despair. The above steps are still needed and you should go through them to gain further insight into how you can improve the unreliable information. This can help to identify why additional resources may be justified in order to make improvements to your ability to measure and report on services.

The information provided in the preceding paragraphs is a good example of proactive CSI at work. In an ideal world, this is the only type of CSI we should need. The real world, however, often provides its share of surprises, which cause us to conduct reactive CSI. The more proactive CSI processes you have in place, the better the chances that there will be fewer surprises. This is because you will have much deeper insight into the performance of services, the performance of your service lifecycle and management practices. Nevertheless, when a reactive CSI initiative is needed due to unforeseen circumstances, rely on the strengths and capabilities you have embedded in your proactive CSI processes to help guide your management of the unexpected issues.

Managing IT resources in small and medium-sized businesses

12

12 Managing IT resources in small and medium-sized businesses

12.1 MANAGING TASKS

Once the IT organization has defined the services it can provide, it can draw up a list of tasks it must carry out. The points to consider are:

- How tasks should be organized and managed
- Which tasks fit naturally together
- The skill mix needed to perform the tasks
- The compromises which can be made to meet the goal of matching tasks with skills.

12.2 MATCHING SKILLS AND TASKS

In the search for quality, management effort is traditionally directed towards the processes underlying service or product delivery. This is amply demonstrated by the high profile of quality management initiatives such as ISO 9000. However, in reality, delivered quality is often more a matter of how well people's skills match those needed by the job: there may be considerable potential for improving quality by matching skills in this way. In an SMB, it is both feasible and desirable to carry out an audit of skills.

12.3 TECHNIQUES FOR ASSESSING SKILLS AND REQUIREMENTS

In order to match staff skills and job requirements, separate assessments are needed of:

- The skills available
- The skills needed to carry out the organization's tasks.

Techniques for assessment might consist of:

- Each person completing a questionnaire designed to reveal features of their personality and their work preferences
- Analysing each job to establish what particular skills or personality features it requires. (This is also a good opportunity to ask the question 'Do we still need to do this job at all?' – probably best expressed as 'What would be the consequences if this were not done?')
- Matching people to jobs (some 'management' interpretation of people's self-assessment might well be necessary).

Making a best-fit match between people and jobs might involve:

- Retraining people for jobs better suited to their skills and preferences
- Restructuring jobs, so that all elements can be carried out efficiently by one person (for example, making sure elements requiring a methodical approach are not mixed with those requiring inspirational thinking).

Even a small improvement in matching skills is likely to be worthwhile in terms of improved performance and staff morale. An exercise which detects a task that would be better dealt with by external resources can release internal staff for tasks they are skilled in. Indeed, skill matching can significantly increase job satisfaction and hence staff retention. The costs of staff turnover are disproportionably high in small organizations and can be a significant factor in meeting

economic targets and efficiency levels. A perfect fit
is never possible, but people will respond positively
to attempts to find jobs which suit them.

Building ITSM in the small and medium-sized business

13

13 Building ITSM in the small and medium-sized business

Now that you have learned how to scale, adapt and perhaps have begun to implement the five lifecycle stages, you should have a stronger sense of what will work for your SMB.

No matter how well designed your lifecycle is, how robust the scaled processes are, unless you have a solid foundation built from the structure of roles and responsibilities, it simply will not work in reality.

Make sure that you assign responsibility to all levels in the IT organization – yes, you read this correctly. Senior management must be part of your ITIL equation even if it is only as the champion. There are graveyards of ITSM initiatives that failed only because this was overlooked, not accepted or thought unimportant.

In organizations with a limited number of IT staff or resources, it is common to see role combinations as a means to cover all ITSM activities. Matching skills of staff to roles is a good way to consider the combinations. Within ITIL, it is possible to group processes and roles that have strong interdependencies with staff positions. Doing so makes scaling processes and activities important, so a realistic workload is shared among staff. One of the advantages in combined roles is the integration of the management of key ITSM activities and a reduced tendency to silo and isolate activities that can lead to confusion and a lack of productive workflow.

13.1 ADAPTING ROLES

This section looks in detail at how to combine and adapt roles within the confines of a small organization.

The major influences on how those roles are actually performed include:

- Staff attitudes, making possible overlap, cross-function working and mutual support (or interference) between ITIL functions
- Restrictions on scope, both because of limitations imposed by staffing and finance, and because the complexity and rigour appropriate for mainstream ITIL functions will not be so necessary.

Additionally, there are aspects of ITSM which apply to all sizes of organization, but which are particularly visible within a small one, where they are also often easier to deal with. Examples include user education and awareness, where a more flexible approach can be taken when dealing with smaller numbers.

In many ways, SMB organizations are in a position to benefit most from increased technology to automate processes, relieving the load on staff. Automation can be a way of offering a full-time process, even when the function itself is only staffed part-time.

13.2 SUGGESTED ROLES

Table 13.1 shows the roles identified in ITIL and organized into the stages of the service lifecycle.

Table 13.1 Roles in ITIL organized by lifecycle stage

Strategy	Design	Transition	Operation	Improvement
Director of service management	Process owner	Service owner	Service desk analyst	CSI manager
Business relationship manager	Design manager	Service transition manager	Service desk supervisor	Service manager
Product manager	IT designer	Service asset manager	Service desk manager	Service owner
Financial manager	IT architect	Configuration manager	Super user	Business process owner
Portfolio manager	Service catalogue manager	Configuration analyst	Technical analyst	
	Service level manager	Configuration administrator	Technical operator	
	Availability manager	CMS tools administrator	IT operations manager	
	IT service continuity manager	Change manager	Shift leader	
	Capacity manager	Change Advisory Board	IT operations analyst	
	Supplier manager	Performance and risk evaluation manager	IT operator	
	Security manager	Service test manager	Application manager	
		Release and deployment manager	Application analyst	
		Release, build and package manager	Incident manager	
			First-line support	
			Second-line support	
			Third-line support	
			Problem manager	

If we think of the core processes and activities that have been recommended for SMB adaptation, there are some fairly obvious roles that could logically be combined.

13.2.1 Roles combined by capability

The core guidance of ITIL describes a variety of generic roles across the service lifecycle. An SMB can take advantage of its capabilities by organizing roles that leverage skill sets across a variety of

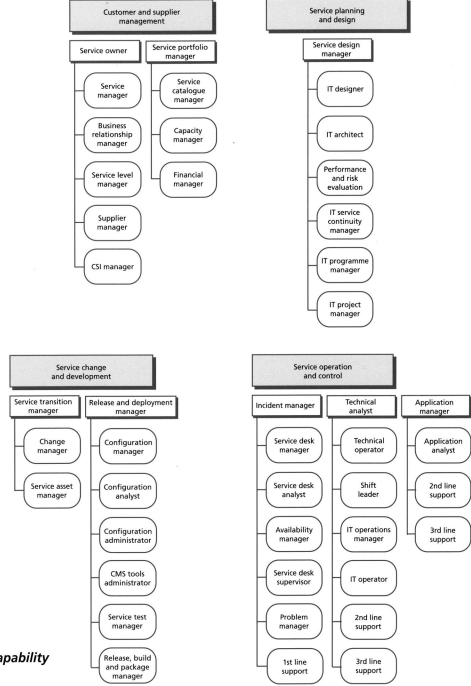

Figure 13.1 Example of capability and role combinations

disciplines. Organizations will often establish their departmental structures by grouping accountability areas together. By using service capability groupings, the SMB can use this approach to help define the necessary roles and set accountability structures. This structure may also be helpful when needing to convince management of the need for additional resources, since the organizational chart structure is more familiar than a list of technical role terms.

Thinking of this from an ITSM capability perspective, the SMB might group sets of roles/ skills that align to patterns in the flow of work. As an example, they could look like the following:

- Operational support and control
- Service change and deployment
- Service planning and design
- Customer and supplier management.

Figure 13.1 shows some key roles and possible combinations, all of which are defined in ITIL core guidance, and which are grouped by service capability. Note that these roles in some cases traverse stages of the lifecycle. There is no reason to segregate lifecycle stages when establishing roles; in fact, having some roles that cross lifecycle stages should be encouraged in order to take a holistic approach.

The preceding examples can be further refined by assigning the lead role or area to an internal staff member but outsourcing some of the subordinate roles. This ensures that overall accountability still rests within the SMB organization, but expertise can be procured as needed.

Each ITSM process or function can be seen as an assembly of component tasks. ITIL explains how these combine into mainstream ITSM roles. However, this structure may need to be reconsidered for SMB organizations. It is important to build a solution that matches the specific requirements of each organization. What follows is suggested for a 'typical' small organization as a starting point for matching actual circumstances and requirements.

The following role descriptions are not meant to include the whole range of responsibilities, but to serve as an overall guide. Refer to the core guidance for a complete view of each of these roles in detail.

13.2.2 Customer and supplier management capability

Role 1 – service owner

The service owner takes on accountability for the overall ITSM and manages some of the primary activities related to quality management. The service owner is the main point of contact for the business customer when negotiating and reviewing service levels and agreements, and for the suppliers and internal technical teams for contracts and operational level agreements.

The processes used to drive the deliverables of this role should not be overly complex, and this is achievable in an SMB with direct access through the service chain.

Combining these roles places the service owner in a logical position to also oversee and manage continual service improvement since they are responsible for the main feedback points from the business and supply chain. The service owner will work closely with all other manager roles, specifically with the service portfolio manager to ensure ongoing analysis of the desired business outcomes is being assessed for changes to the delivery of services.

The service owner should possess management level skills and be considered a senior member of the IT organization.

Role 2 – service portfolio manager

The service portfolio manager assumes most primary planning activities and has accountability for ensuring the service portfolio is current and reflects the service pipeline and catalogue. The service portfolio manager is a liaison for all management positions in the IT organization. Strong communication, planning and fiscal management skills will be required to fulfil this role.

The service portfolio manager will be the predominant role involved in business-planning activities and work closely with the service owner in establishing service and contractual agreements.

13.2.3 Service planning and design capability

Role 3 – service design manager

The process and activities within the service design stage of the lifecycle is an area where outsourcing opportunities should be considered. This is due to the highly specialized skills needed at cyclical points in the service lifecycle, rather than on a daily basis, and so outsourcing may be an economical way to access the specialists, rather than training and maintaining them in house.

If this role is outsourced, supplier management will need to be a very mature practice to link the service portfolio management (SPM) and decisions on core and service level packages (SLPs) to the service design activities. Investments in people, processes, products and technology should be discussed between all roles, but in particular the service design and service portfolio managers and the service owner.

This role should include the design of processes, technical architecture, continuity and risk evaluation. The role is well positioned to consider and accomplish these things before services are built, and will involve project management skills and activities.

13.2.4 Service change and deployment capability

Role 4 – service transition manager

The roles included within this area are critical in any size of organization. In Figure 13.1, the service transition manager role is shown aligned with the release and deployment manager since there will be crossover in most of the process activities during the development and transition of services from the design to operation stages.

The service transition manager role is responsible for service asset and change management and the ancillary activities that surround this. Since service asset and change management can consume a large amount of the daily operational activity, it is wise to not overburden this area with a lot of subordinate roles.

Role 5 – release and deployment manager

This role should focus on all processes and activities that have dependency on the transition stage of the lifecycle. The release and deployment manager role has responsibility for planning, build, test and deployment of release packages and the associated configuration activities of identification, control, accounting and verification. In a small organization, process and activities should be streamlined, and impose a manageable level of control and approval. The use of third-party suppliers should be encouraged where infrequent need is the general rule.

13.2.5 Service operation and control capability

Role 6 – incident manager

Whether or not an SMB chooses to outsource its service desk, second- or third-tier support, ownership and accountability of incident management should remain internal. Service disruptions affect the business customer and the coordination and control of service response, and restoration should be overseen by someone in the SMB organization. Incident management is best assigned as a full-time role and can be coupled with problem management using clear workflow which segregates these two activities.

Role 7 – technical analyst

In a small organization the role of technical analyst will perform a wide range of functions across the operational spectrum. While this is a key role involving numerous specialist skills, a realistic workload must be a priority. Depending on the variety of skills required, it may be worth the investment to have more than one individual in this role. The technical knowledge needed in this role can offer opportunities to link to many of the ITIL processes such as:

- Release and deployment management
- Build and test
- Early life support
- Change management
- IT service continuity management
- Service evaluation
- Tiered support
- Problem management.

Role 8 – application manager

This role is most often associated with business applications. Application managers are responsible for managing applications throughout their lifecycle. The application management function supports and maintains operational applications and also plays an important role in the design, testing and improvement of applications that form part of IT services. Application management is usually divided into departments based on the application portfolio of the organization, thus allowing easier specialization and focused support. In many organizations, application management departments have staff who perform daily operations for those applications.

In a small organization, the application manager will generally have responsibility for all applications and will require a wide array of skills and knowledge. This role will interface with most of the service lifecycle areas from design to operation.

14

Tools and advice

14 Tools and advice

14.1 ITSM SOFTWARE TOOLS

In any organization of whatever size, a workable ITSM solution requires some level of automation. For a small SMB, a modest investment can make considerable improvement in the function of ITSM, by removing onerous and labour-intensive workflows. Every organization should consider software tools as an enhancement to solid practice, not a replacement for it.

The use of office productivity tools such as spreadsheets, word-processing templates and automated forms may comprise some ITSM enhancing capability initially while the SMB becomes familiar with practices, processes and workflows and works to adapt them to its needs. More robust and integrated software solutions can be well worth the investment in the long run.

Today, there are many options to choose from, which offer the basic and most commonly used processes. Web-based, zero-footprint and open-source tools are becoming increasingly popular in the marketplace.

The first thing to consider is the type of automation that makes sense and then how scalable the technology is as your practices become more robust and mature.

Managing services through the lifecycle requires some good basic information management, and the SMB should consider these as a starting point:

- Incident recording and tracking
- Change and service request recording and tracking

- Event monitoring and control
- Configuration item recording, updating and reporting
- Service measurement.

The latest integrated service management tools are comprehensive, relevant and impressive. They can also be expensive and are often designed for use in larger enterprises. Processes do need tool support, but to deliver benefits, the tools must be:

- Matched to the requirements
- Installed and populated appropriately (in accordance with the specific requirements of the organization)
- Matched to process maturity (for example, no tool, however sophisticated, can support incident management if there is an inadequate incident management process).

What this means is that an SMB starting from zero will begin to introduce simple improvements and start with immature processes. Tools designed to support mature processes may not be well matched to requirements, but will require serious investment, both to purchase and license, and also in terms of staff resources to administer. Furthermore, as the processes mature, the match between any tool and the processes it supports will decrease, and the tool will need to be restructured or replaced.

So, for a small organization starting out, it might well be more sensible to begin very simply, for example by recording calls in a relatively simple database. For an organization that had no central logging point before, this constitutes a significant step forward at minimal cost. More importantly, it carries low overhead and can be thrown away when the organization is ready to move to the next phase when a more sophisticated solution is justified.

Example 1

An organization is 'sold' a sophisticated integrated service management product, which rightly claimed to support ITIL processes. Since there is minimal ITIL knowledge within the organization, the product is installed 'out of the box'. Support from the supplier is available but charged on a daily basis and, since the tool was expensive, little extra money is available. The product works, but lack of mature processes means only some 10% of the features are used – effectively the product is being used to log and track calls and assign incidents to second- and third-line support. Some analysis of affected components/user areas is possible, but not well matched to the organization's current organizational structure and purchasing methods. (Like many companies, the organizational structure evolves rapidly and changes frequently.)

Example 2

An organization sets out to introduce a service desk to capture calls and information. It takes on a computer science student for the summer vacation and uses them to develop a simple Access database to record basic details on the calls they take and how they react to them. The first version has some troubles, but the student reworks it and they are able to record all calls and log them, know where the call has been assigned and track progress through to second- and third-line support. Some analysis is possible, but it is hard to match it to the current structure of the organization.

In these two scenarios, both organizations have the same amount of management information from their support tools, but one has spent more money and is locked into a route whereas the other can now look at the situation afresh with the knowledge it has learned through hands-on experience, and specify its requirements for the next stage of its ITIL maturity programme.

Even in the smallest of organizations, introducing a software tool should be treated as a project which establishes the need for the tool, justifies its acquisition and makes sure that the right resources are put into installing it. The need for a controlled justification and implementation is not dependent on the size or scale of either the software or the organization. The project's purpose is to implement changes to the processes, not just to produce revised software. This means that even a simple database installation needs to be carefully implemented, taking the views of all areas of the business that might be affected.

The informal nature of SMB organizations makes it tempting to think that service management tools can be implemented quickly at minimal cost. This is simply not true. There are some established maxims for introducing tools, which apply to all kinds of support tools in all sizes of IT organization:

- The cost of the tool is more than its purchase price. Costs to consider after the initial investment include:
  - Preparing data for initial upload
  - Staff training and familiarization – in addition to basic training, staff will need practice before they are competent

- Developing and implementing any revised processes that the tool either requires or permits
■ Free-to-use shareware with no support might turn out to be more expensive over time than commercial software with good support included
■ Introducing a new function will not save money; a new, comprehensive service management tool will make new processes and new information possible. This may improve services to customers. However, in the short term at least, introducing new functions will need extra time and money
■ Automated chaos is just faster chaos. Before installing a tool, it is always worth spending time to try to improve current practices. For example, if configuration inventory figures are inaccurate, a state-of-the-art configuration management database (CMDB) will just provide a very detailed record of items that don't exist.

If you use external suppliers, it is wise to discuss the kind of ITSM information that you expect to have access to (and give suppliers access to). A common cause of problems between IT organizations and their suppliers is not being able to integrate internal and supplier technologies or the information that needs to pass between them to properly manage end-to-end services.

Many of the tools available today offer a variety of data formats, so be certain that whatever you invest in will provide information in the common industry-standard data formats. This ensures that as suppliers change, you will not have to re-tool in order to maintain and integrate service information.

A common approach in SMBs is to rely on providers who offer software as a service (SaaS).

This reduces the overhead of purchasing and managing software and can offer a cost-effective way to make use of more sophisticated software in the market, while taking advantage of the cost avoidance.

14.2 KNOWLEDGE BASE

While a small organization will neither be able to afford sophisticated knowledge-based software, nor the major administrative overheads that larger organizations might manage, there is still much benefit from recording learned information in a reusable fashion, for example through the organization's shared folders on the network.

Using ITSM tools to help build a knowledge base is an added benefit to existing investment. Key features (which are relatively easy to implement) are possible, such as:

■ Consistent methods of capturing incident data – essential for matching similar incidents, should they recur, and feeding to problem-management knowledge
■ Accessible repository of diagnostic scripts for service desk staff use
■ Repository of known errors and workaround information
■ Repository of documented requests for change (RFCs) and SLA information.

Even in small organizations, the knowledge base will benefit from the inclusion of the change schedule, workarounds and known errors etc. The repository can also include service portfolio and catalogue information, and can also contain FAQs and hints and tips to assist in customer self-help.

The smaller the organization, the higher the percentage of the budget a support tool is likely to require. This makes it harder for small organizations to justify tools, and especially to justify an integrated service management tool rather than one which only does a part of the job. Nevertheless, even the smallest of organizations will probably still benefit from using an integrated service support tool, because:

- By combining many functions in a single tool, the tool should provide:
  - A cheaper option in the long run than several different tools
  - A single learning curve, allowing savings to accrue more quickly
  - An integrated picture of incidents and errors, allowing service desk staff to resolve more incidents without escalation
  - An economy of scale by using the tools for extended functions outside of IT services
  - Greater data integrity, since data is held once and shared by all users
- The procedures established will minimize dependence on one or two individuals
- Holding information electronically rather than on paper is much safer and cheaper, with important implications for contingency and back-up. Copying an electronic database many times is trivial; copying a paper data bank is almost impossible.

14.3   WHERE TO GO FOR ADVICE

Staff in SMB organizations often feel isolated; compared to larger organizations they have fewer fellow IT professionals within their daily environment. (The benefit, of course, is that they are more likely to be in regular professional and social contact with non-IT staff, helping to develop a wider and more balanced view of their role

within the organization.) There are sources of advice and comparison available. Some potential contacts are given here:

- **IT Service Management Forum (itSMF)**   The itSMF is an independent, not-for-profit organization dedicated to the development and promotion of best practice in ITSM. It is wholly owned and principally run by its members. There are chapters in more than 50 countries, and an international coordinating body, the itSMF International. All itSMF chapters provide a mechanism for local members to meet and discuss mutual concerns and ideas. Many chapters have specialist groups for small organizations.

  Information about itSMF chapters is available through the website www.itsmf.com

- **Other IT organizations**   Your problems are rarely unique. Similar IT organizations are likely to have encountered similar problems. Consult with more than one such organization. Identify elements of their approaches best suited to your own environment. Formulate an approach and discuss with these organizations. An itSMF chapter (see previous point) in your area can often make connections and contacts, as can industry user groups (where an IT sub-group may be operating or worth initiating) and local business associations
- **Consultancy**   Consider the use of external consultants. Once again, solicit recommendations from managers of other IT organizations
- **Regulatory bodies**   Information concerning specialist areas can often be obtained from government or other regulatory organizations.

Appendix A: Service catalogue example

Appendix A: Service catalogue example

The service catalogue is a key document containing valuable information on the complete set of services offered. It should preferably be stored as a set of 'service' CIs within a CMS, maintained under change management. As it is such a valuable set of information it should be available to anyone within the organization. Every new service should immediately be entered into the service catalogue once its initial definition of requirements has been documented and agreed. So as well as the information below, the service catalogue should record the status of every service, through the stages of its defined lifecycle.

Table A.1 Service catalogue example

Service name	Service description	Service type	Supporting services	Business owner(s)	Business unit(s)	Service manager(s)	Business impact	Business priority	SLA	Service hours	Business contacts	Escalation contacts	Service reports	Service reviews	Security rating
Service 1															
Service 2															
Service 3															
Service 4															

Appendix B: Examples of an SLA and OLA

B

Appendix B: Examples of an SLA and OLA

This appendix contains examples of a service level agreement (SLA) and an operational level agreement (OLA) and their contents. It is not recommended that every SLA or OLA should necessarily contain all of the sections listed within the following sample documents. It is suggested that these areas are considered when preparing document templates, but that they are only incorporated into the actual documents themselves where they are appropriate and relevant. So the following outlines should only be considered as guidelines or checklists.

SERVICE LEVEL AGREEMENT (SLA – SAMPLE)

This agreement is made between.............................
.......................and.......................................

The agreement covers the provision and support of the ABC services which..... (brief service description).

This agreement remains valid for 12 months from the (date) until (date). The agreement will be reviewed annually. Minor changes may be recorded on the form at the end of the agreement, providing they are mutually endorsed by the two parties and managed through the change management process.

Signatories:

Name.....................Position...................Date...............

Name.....................Position...................Date...............

Service description

The ABC service consists of.... (a fuller description to include key business functions, deliverables and all relevant information to describe the service and its scale, impact and priority for the business).

Scope of the agreement

What is covered within the agreement and what is excluded?

Service hours

A description of the hours that the customers can expect the service to be available (e.g. 7 x 24 x 365, 08:00 to 18:00 – Monday to Friday).

Special conditions for exceptions (e.g. weekends, public holidays) and procedures for requesting service extensions (who to contact – normally the service desk – and what notice periods are required).

This could include a service calendar or reference to a service calendar.

Details of any pre-agreed maintenance or housekeeping slots, if these impact on service hours, together with details of how any other potential outages must be negotiated and agreed – by whom and notice periods etc.

Procedures for requesting permanent changes to service hours.

Service availability

The target availability levels that the IT service provider will seek to deliver within the agreed service hours. Availability targets within agreed service hours, normally expressed as percentages (e.g. 99.5%), measurement periods, method and calculations must be stipulated. This figure may be expressed for the overall service, underpinning services and critical components or all three. However, it is difficult to relate such simplistic percentage availability figures to service quality, or to customer business activities. It is therefore often better to try to measure service unavailability in terms of the customer's inability to conduct its business activities. For example, 'sales are immediately affected by a failure of IT to provide an adequate POS support service'. This strong link between the IT service and the customer's business processes is a sign of maturity in both the SLM and the availability management processes.

Agreed details of how and at what point this will be measured and reported, and over what agreed period, should also be documented.

Reliability

The maximum number of service breaks that can be tolerated within an agreed period (may be defined either as number of breaks e.g. four per annum, or as a mean time between failures (MTBF) or mean time between systems incidents (MTBSI)).

Definition of what constitutes a 'break' and how these will be monitored and recorded.

Customer support

Details of how to contact the service desk, the hours it will be available, the hours support is available and what to do outside these hours to obtain assistance (e.g. on-call support, third-party assistance etc.) must be documented. The SLA may also include reference to internet/intranet self-help and/or incident logging. Metrics and measurements should be included such as telephone call answer targets (number of rings, missed calls etc.)

Targets for incident response times (how long will it be before someone starts to assist the customer – may include travelling time etc.)

A definition is needed of 'response' – is it a telephone call back to the customer or a site visit? – as appropriate.

Arrangements for requesting support extensions, including required notice periods (e.g. request must be made to the service desk by 12 noon for an evening extension, by 12 noon on Thursday for a weekend extension).

Note. Both incident response and resolution times will be based on whatever incident impact/priority codes are used – details of the classification of incidents should also be included here.

Note. In some cases, it may be appropriate to reference out to third-party contacts and contracts and OLAs – but not as a way of diverting responsibility.

Contact points and escalation

Details of the contacts within each of the parties involved in the agreement and the escalation processes and contact points. This should also include the definition of a complaint and procedure for managing complaints.

Service performance

Details of the expected responsiveness of the IT service (e.g. target workstation response times for average, or maximum workstation response times, sometimes expressed as a percentile – e.g. 95% within two seconds), details of expected service throughput on which targets are based, and any thresholds that would invalidate the targets).

This should include indication of likely traffic volumes, throughput activity, constraints and dependencies (e.g. the number of transactions to be processed, number of concurrent users, and amount of data to be transmitted over the network). This is important so that performance issues that have been caused by excessive throughput outside the terms of the agreement may be identified.

Batch turnaround times

If appropriate, details of any batch turnaround times, completion times and key deliverables, including times for delivery of input and the time and place for delivery of output where appropriate.

Functionality (if appropriate)

Details of the minimal functionality to be provided and the number of errors of particular types that can be tolerated before the SLA is breached. Should include severity levels and the reporting period.

Change management

Brief mention of and/or reference out to the organization's change management procedures that must be followed – just to reinforce compliance. Also targets for approving, handling and implementing RFCs, usually based on the category or urgency/priority of the change, should also be included and details of any known changes that will impact on the agreement, if any.

Service continuity

Brief mention of and/or reference out to the organization's service continuity plans, together with details of how the SLA might be affected or reference to a separate continuity SLA, containing details of any diminished or amended service targets should a disaster situation occur. Details of any specific responsibilities on both sides (e.g.

data backup, off-site storage). Also details of the invocation of plans and coverage of any security issues, particularly any customer responsibilities (e.g. coordination of business activities, business documentation, backup of freestanding PCs, password changes).

Security

Brief mention of and/or reference out to the organization's security policy (covering issues such as password controls, security violations, unauthorized software, viruses etc.). Details of any specific responsibilities on both sides (e.g. virus protection, firewalls).

Printing

Details of any special conditions relating to printing or printers (e.g. print distribution details, notification of large centralized print runs, or handling of any special high-value stationery).

Responsibilities

Details of the responsibilities of the various parties involved within the service and their agreed responsibilities, including the service provider, the customer and the users.

Charging (if applicable)

Details of any charging formulas used, charging periods, or reference out to charging policy documents, together with invoicing procedures and payment conditions etc. must be included. This should also include details of any financial penalties or bonuses that will be paid if service targets do not meet expectations. What the penalties/bonuses will be and how they will be calculated, agreed and collected/paid (more appropriate for third-party situations). If the SLA covers an outsourcing relationship, charges should be detailed in an appendix as they are often covered by commercial in-confidence provisions.

It should be noted that penalty clauses can create their own difficulties. They can prove a barrier to partnerships if unfairly invoked on a technicality and can also make service provider staff unwilling to admit to mistakes for fear of penalties being imposed. This can, unless used properly, be a barrier to developing effective relationships and problem solving.

Service reporting and reviewing

The content, frequency, content, timing and distribution of service reports, and the frequency of associated service review meetings. Also details of how and when SLAs and the associated service targets will be reviewed and possibly revised, including who will be involved and in what capacity.

Glossary

Explanation of any unavoidable abbreviations or terminology used, to assist customer understanding.

Amendment sheet

To include a record of any agreed amendments, with details of amendments, dates and signatories. It should also contain details of a complete change history of the document and its revisions.

It should be noted that the SLA contents given above are examples only. They should not be regarded as exhaustive or mandatory, but they provide a good starting point.

OPERATIONAL LEVEL AGREEMENT (OLA – SAMPLE)

This agreement is made between............................. ....and.......................................

The agreement covers the provision of the support service providing..... (brief service description).

This agreement remains valid for 12 months from the (date) until (date).

The agreement will be reviewed annually. Minor changes may be recorded on the form at the end of the agreement, providing they are mutually endorsed by the two parties and managed through the change management process.

Signatories

Name....................Position...................Date..............

Name....................Position...................Date..............

Details of previous amendments

Support service description

Comprehensive explanation and details of the support service being provided.

Scope of the agreement

What is covered within the agreement and what is excluded?

Service hours

A description of the hours for which the support service is provided.

Service targets

The targets for the provision of the support service and the reporting and reviewing processes and frequency.

Contact points and escalation

Details of the contacts within each of the parties involved within the agreement and the escalation processes and contact points.

Service desk and incident response times and responsibilities

The responsibilities and targets agreed for the progress and resolution of incidents and support of the service desk.

Problem response times and responsibilities

The responsibilities and targets agreed for the progress and resolution of problems.

Change management

The responsibilities and targets agreed for the progress and implementation of changes.

Release management

The responsibilities and targets agreed for the progress and implementation of releases.

Configuration management

The responsibilities for the ownership, provision and maintenance of accurate configuration management information.

Information security management

The responsibilities and targets agreed for the support of the security policy(s) and the information security management process.

Availability management

Responsibility for ensuring that all components within their support domain are managed and supported to meet and continue to meet all of the service and component availability targets.

Service continuity management

Responsibility for ensuring that all components within their support domain have up-to-date and tested recovery plans that support agreed and documented business requirements. This should include assistance with the technical assessment of risk and its subsequent management and mitigation.

Capacity management

Responsibility for supporting the needs of the capacity management process within the agreed scope of their technical domain.

Service level management

Assistance with the definition and agreement of appropriate targets within SLAs, SLRs and OLAs, concerning components within the scope of their technical domain.

Supplier management

Assistance with the management of contracts and suppliers, again principally within the scope of their technical domain.

Provision of information

The provision and maintenance of accurate information, including financial data for all components within the agreed scope of their technical domain.

Glossary

Explanation of any unavoidable abbreviations or terminology used, to assist understanding of terms contained within the agreement.

Amendment sheet

To include a record of any agreed amendments, with details of amendments, dates and signatories. It should also contain details of a complete change history of the document and its revisions.

Further information

Further information

ABOUT OGC

The UK government recognized very early on the significance of best practice and created initiatives to identify efficient, successful and reliable approaches to various management disciplines. The Office of Government Commerce, as an office of HM Treasury, has played a vital role in developing methodologies, processes and frameworks, and establishing these as best practice. These include ITIL, which is now the most widely accepted approach to service management in the world; PRINCE2, a world-leading project management methodology, Managing Successful Programmes (MSP™) and Management of Risk (M_o_R®).

E-mail: ServiceDesk@ogc.gsi.gov.uk

www.ogc.gov.uk

Further information on ITIL can be found at www.itil-officialsite.com

ABOUT TSO

TSO (The Stationery Office) has 200 years' experience of providing publishing and digital information solutions to the public sector. It specializes in the creation, production and distribution of information in print, online and in electronic formats. TSO is Britain's largest publisher by output, publishing 15,000 printed and electronic products each year.

TSO has a long history of working with OGC, and is the official publisher of its best-practice guidance, managing various refresh projects on behalf of OGC.

For more information on TSO's publications, please e-mail or visit TSO's website:

customer.services@tso.co.uk

www.tso.co.uk

ABOUT APM GROUP

The APM Group is a global business providing accreditation and certification services. Through its international network of Accredited Consultancy and Training Organizations (ACTO), the APM Group helps end-users develop their professional skills and organizations improve their processes through the adoption of worldwide best practice.

As the official accreditor, the APM Group works closely with the UK Office of Government Commerce and TSO, running global accreditation schemes in ITIL; PRINCE2; MSP; Portfolio, Programme and Project Offices (P3O®); and M_o_R.

E-mail: servicedesk@apmgroup.co.uk

www.apmgroup.co.uk

ABOUT ITSMF

The IT Service Management Forum (itSMF) is an independent and internationally recognized forum for IT service management professionals worldwide. This not-for-profit organization is a prominent player in the ongoing development and promotion of IT service management best practice, standards and qualifications, and has been since 1991.

Globally, itSMF now boasts more than 6,000 member companies, blue-chip and public-sector alike, covering in excess of 70,000 individuals spread over 40+ international chapters.

Each chapter is a separate legal entity and is largely autonomous. The forum itSMF International provides an overall steering and support function to existing and emerging chapters.

www.itsmfi.org

OGC'S ITIL PUBLICATIONS PORTFOLIO

Titles published by TSO, the official ITIL publisher, are given below. Full details of the range of material published under the ITIL banner, including the formats, can also be found at:

www.best-management-practice.com/Publications-Library/IT-Service-Management-ITIL

The ITIL lifecycle publications suite (core publications)

The core ITIL titles have been commissioned and structured to be read as a series of five titles, each building on the work of the other. As the five core titles reflect the lifecycle of services, their appeal encompasses the entire spectrum of people involved at any stage of the framework.

The ITIL lifecycle publications suite comprises:

- *Service Strategy* (TSO, 2007)
- *Service Design* (TSO, 2007)
- *Service Transition* (TSO, 2007)
- *Service Operation* (TSO, 2007)
- *Continual Service Improvement* (TSO, 2007)

The Official Introduction to the ITIL Service Lifecycle

This publication is your gateway to ITIL. It explains the basic concept of ITSM and the place of ITIL, introducing the new lifecycle model, which puts into context all the familiar ITIL processes from the earlier books. This title introduces ITSM and ITIL, explains why the service lifecycle approach is best practice in today's ITSM environment, and makes a persuasive case for change.

The Official Introduction to the ITIL Service Lifecycle (TSO, 2007)

Key element guides

Written by the original authoring team for the ITIL V3 Project, these key element guides are a handy and portable set of reference guides to the core ITIL lifecycle publications. They discuss ITIL and its evolution and the need for the service lifecycle approach. The titles examine what is meant by a best-practice framework, how this relates to 'common practice', and what compliance means. The main focus of each of the key element guides is to provide an overview of the principles, objectives, key elements, roles, responsibilities, challenges and key lessons for each of the five elements of the service lifecycle. There is a key element guide for each lifecycle stage:

- *Key Element Guide Service Strategy* (TSO, 2008)
- *Key Element Guide Service Design* (TSO, 2008)
- *Key Element Guide Service Transition* (TSO, 2008)
- *Key Element Guide Service Operation* (TSO, 2008)
- *Key Element Guide Continual Service Improvement* (TSO, 2008)

Passing your ITIL Foundation Exam – the Official Study Aid

Endorsed by the APM Group, the official ITIL accreditor, this publication is suitable for those taking the foundation exam. It provides an overview of the purpose, objectives and format of the examination, and offers a top-level introduction to understanding the service lifecycle and each of its five components. It also contains a mock exam with an answer key and rationale.

Passing your ITIL Foundation Exam (TSO, 2007)

ITIL V3 Foundation Handbook

Produced in conjunction with itSMF UK, the *ITIL V3 Foundation Handbook* performs a dual role. It's a quick management-level reference tool for those interested in ITIL V3, and also covers the full content of the ITIL V3 foundation syllabus, providing an ideal revision aid. It offers basic information around each process and function in the lifecycle, with cross-referencing to the core books for more in-depth reading.

ITIL V3 Foundation Handbook, second edition (TSO, 2009)

Building an ITIL-based Service Management Department

ITIL concentrates on describing IT service management processes, functions and roles but does not describe how to build a department to run and manage those processes, leaving the question 'How can I structure my organization to most effectively support ITIL service management?' This publication explains in a structured and logical manner how to build an ITIL-based service management department that will both support and supplement those processes.

Building an ITIL-based Service Management Department (TSO, 2008)

Abbreviations and glossary

Abbreviations

AM	availability management
BCM	business continuity management
BIA	business impact analysis
BRM	business relationship manager
CAB	Change Advisory Board
CI	configuration item
CMDB	configuration management database
CMS	configuration management system
COBIT	Control Objectives for Information and related Technology
CSI	continual service improvement
ELS	early life support
EM	event management
eTOM	enhanced Telecom Operations Map
IEC	International Electrotechnical Commission
ISM	information security management
ISO	international organization for standardization
IT	information technology
ITIL	IT infrastructure library
ITSCM	IT service continuity management
ITSM	IT service management
itSMF	IT Service Management Forum
LSA	local systems administrator
MTBF	mean time between failures
MTBSI	mean time between service incidents
OGC	Office of Government Commerce
OLA	operational level agreement
OPSI	Office of Public Sector Information
PBA	pattern of business activity
PMBOK	Project Management Body of Knowledge

PRINCE2	PRojects IN Controlled Environments – a standard methodology for managing projects
QA	quality assurance
RACI	Responsible–Accountable–Consulted–Informed
RFC	request for change
ROI	return on investment
SaaS	software as a service
SACM	service asset and configuration management
SDP	service design package
Six Sigma	a business management strategy
SKMS	service knowledge management system
SLA	service level agreement
SLM	service level management
SLP	service level package
SLR	service level requirement
SMB	small or medium-sized business
SOX	Sarbanes-Oxley (US legislation)
SPM	service portfolio management
SPOC	single point of contact
TOGAF	The Open Group architecture framework
UP	user profile
VBF	vital business function
VOI	value on investment

Glossary

The publication names included in parentheses after the name of a term identify where a reader can find more information about that term. This is either because the term is primarily used by that publication or because additional useful information about that term can be found there. Terms without a publication name associated with them may be used generally by several publications, or may not be defined in any greater detail than can be found in the glossary; i.e. we only point readers to places where they can expect to expand on their knowledge or to see a greater context. Terms with multiple publication names are covered in multiple publications.

Where the definition of a term includes another term, those related terms are **emboldened**. This is designed to help the reader with their understanding by pointing them to additional definitions that are part of the original term they were interested in. The form 'See also Term X, Term Y' is used at the end of a definition where an important related term is not used within the text of the definition itself.

access management

(*Service Operation*) The **process** responsible for allowing users to make use of IT services, data, or other assets. Access management helps to protect the confidentiality, integrity and availability of assets by ensuring that only authorized users are able to access or modify the assets. Access management is sometimes referred to as rights management or identity management.

accounting

(*Service Strategy*) The **process** responsible for identifying actual costs of delivering IT services, comparing these with budgeted costs and managing variance from the budget.

application

Software that provides **functions** which are required by an IT service. Each application may be part of more than one IT service. An application runs on one or more servers or clients. *See also* application management.

application management

(*Service Design, Service Operation*) The **function** responsible for managing applications throughout their lifecycle.

availability management

(*Service Design*) The **process** responsible for defining, analysing, planning, measuring and improving all aspects of the availability of IT services. Availability management is responsible for ensuring that all IT infrastructure, processes, tools, roles etc. are appropriate for the agreed service level targets for availability.

budgeting

The activity of predicting and controlling the spending of money. Consists of a periodic negotiation cycle to set future budgets (usually annual) and the day-to-day **monitoring** and adjusting of current budgets.

business continuity management

(*Service Design*) The business process responsible for managing risks that could seriously affect the business. BCM safeguards the interests of key stakeholders, reputation, brand and value-creating activities. The BCM process involves reducing risks to an acceptable level and planning for the recovery of business processes should a disruption to the business occur. BCM sets the objectives, scope and requirements for IT service continuity management.

business impact analysis

(*Service Strategy*) BIA is the activity in business continuity management (BCM) that identifies vital business functions (VBFs) and their dependencies. These dependencies may include suppliers, people, other business processes, IT services etc. BIA defines the recovery requirements for IT services. These requirements include recovery time objectives, recovery point objectives and minimum service level targets for each IT service.

capability

(*Service Strategy*) The ability of an organization, person, **process, application, configuration item** or IT service to carry out an activity. Capabilities are intangible assets of an organization. *See also* resource.

capacity management

(*Service Design*) The **process** responsible for ensuring that the capacity of IT services and the IT infrastructure is able to deliver agreed service level targets in a cost-effective and timely manner. Capacity management considers all resources required to deliver the IT service and plans for short-, medium- and long-term business requirements.

change management

(*Service Transition*) The **process** responsible for controlling the lifecycle of all changes. The primary objective of change management is to enable beneficial changes to be made, with minimum disruption to IT services.

COBIT

Control Objectives for Information and related Technology provides guidance and best practice for the management of IT processes. COBIT is published by the IT Governance Institute. See www.isaca.org for more information.

configuration item

(*Service Transition*) Any component that needs to be managed in order to deliver an IT service. Information about each CI is recorded in a configuration record within the **configuration management system** and is maintained throughout its lifecycle by **configuration management**. CIs are under the control of **change management**. CIs typically include IT services, hardware, software, buildings, people and formal documentation such as **process** documentation and **service level agreements**.

configuration management

(*Service Transition*) The **process** responsible for maintaining information about **configuration items** required to deliver an IT service, including their relationships. This information is managed throughout the lifecycle of the CI. Configuration management is part of an overall **service asset and configuration management** process.

configuration management system

(*Service Transition*) A set of tools and databases that are used to manage an IT service provider's configuration data. The CMS also includes information about **incidents**, problems, known errors, changes and releases; and may contain data about employees, suppliers, locations, business units, customers and users. The CMS includes tools for collecting, storing, managing, updating and presenting data about all **configuration items** and their relationships. The CMS is maintained by **configuration management** and is used by all IT service management processes.

continual service improvement

(*Continual Service Improvement*) A stage in the lifecycle of an IT service and the title of one of the core ITIL publications. Continual service improvement is responsible for managing improvements to IT service management processes and IT services. The performance of the IT service provider is continually measured and improvements are made to processes, IT services and IT infrastructure in order to increase efficiency, effectiveness and cost-effectiveness.

event management

(*Service Operation*) The **process** responsible for managing events throughout their lifecycle. Event management is one of the main activities of IT operations.

function

A team or group of people and the tools they use to carry out one or more processes or activities. For example, the **service desk**.

The term 'function' also has two other meanings:

- An intended purpose of a **configuration item**, person, team, **process** or IT service. For example, one function of an e-mail service may be to store and forward outgoing messages; one function of a business process may be to dispatch goods to customers
- To perform the intended purpose correctly, as in 'The computer is functioning.'

incident

(*Service Operation*) An unplanned interruption to an IT service or reduction in the quality of an IT service. Failure of a **configuration item** that has not yet affected service is also an incident. For example, failure of one disk from a mirror set.

incident management

(*Service Operation*) The **process** responsible for managing the lifecycle of all **incidents**. The primary objective of incident management is to return the IT service to customers as quickly as possible.

information security management

(*Service Design*) The **process** that ensures the confidentiality, integrity and availability of an organization's assets, information, data and IT services. Information security management usually forms part of an organizational approach to security management that has a wider scope than the IT service provider, and includes handling of paper, buildings access, phone calls etc. for the entire organization.

IT operations management

(*Service Operation*) The **function** within an IT service provider that performs the daily activities needed to manage IT services and the supporting IT infrastructure. IT operations management includes IT operations control and facilities management.

IT service continuity management

(*Service Design*) The **process** responsible for managing risks that could seriously affect IT services. ITSCM ensures that the IT service provider can always provide minimum agreed service levels, by reducing the risk to an acceptable level and planning for the recovery of IT services. ITSCM should be designed to support business continuity management (BCM).

knowledge management

(*Service Transition*) The **process** responsible for gathering, analysing, storing and sharing knowledge and information within an organization. The primary purpose of knowledge management is to improve efficiency by reducing the need to rediscover knowledge.

monitoring

(*Service Operation*) Repeated observation of a **configuration item**, IT service or **process** to detect events and to ensure that the current status is known.

operational level agreement

(*Service Design, Continual Service Improvement*) An agreement between an IT service provider and another part of the same organization. An OLA supports the IT service provider's delivery of IT services to customers. The OLA defines the goods or services to be provided and the responsibilities of both parties. For example, there could be an OLA:

- Between the IT service provider and a procurement department to obtain hardware in agreed times

- Between the **service desk** and a support group to provide **incident** resolution in agreed times.

See also service level agreement.

problem management

(*Service Operation*) The **process** responsible for managing the lifecycle of all problems. The primary objectives of problem management are to prevent **incidents** from happening, and to minimize the impact of incidents that cannot be prevented.

process

A structured set of activities designed to accomplish a specific objective. A process takes one or more defined inputs and turns them into defined outputs. A process may include any of the roles, responsibilities, tools and management controls required to reliably deliver the outputs. A process may define policies, standards, guidelines, activities and work instructions if they are needed.

RACI

A model used to help define roles and responsibilities. RACI stands for Responsible, Accountable, Consulted and Informed.

release and deployment management

(*Service Transition*) The **process** responsible for both release management and deployment.

request fulfilment

(*Service Operation*) The **process** responsible for managing the lifecycle of all service requests.

resource

(*Service Strategy*) A generic term that includes IT infrastructure, people, money or anything else that might help to deliver an IT service. Resources are considered to be assets of an organization. *See also* capability.

return on investment

(*Service Strategy, Continual Service Improvement*) A measurement of the expected benefit of an investment. In the simplest sense it is the net profit of an investment divided by the net worth of the assets invested. See also value on investment.

service asset and configuration management

(*Service Transition*) The **process** responsible for both **configuration management** and asset management.

service catalogue

(*Service Design*) A database or structured document with information about all live IT services, including those available for deployment. The service catalogue is the only part of the **service portfolio** published to customers, and is used to support the sale and delivery of IT services. The service catalogue includes information about deliverables, prices, contact points, ordering and request processes.

service design

(*Service Design*) A stage in the lifecycle of an IT service. Service design includes a number of **processes** and **functions** and is the title of one of the core ITIL publications.

service desk

(*Service Operation*) The single point of contact between the service provider and the users. A typical service desk manages **incidents** and service requests, and also handles communication with the users.

service knowledge management system

(*Service Transition*) A set of tools and databases that are used to manage knowledge and information. The SKMS includes the **configuration management system**, as well as other tools and databases. The SKMS stores, manages, updates and presents all information that an IT service provider needs to manage the full lifecycle of IT services.

service level agreement

(*Service Design, Continual Service Improvement*) An agreement between an IT service provider and a customer. The SLA describes the IT service, documents service level targets, and specifies the responsibilities of the IT service provider and the customer. A single SLA may cover multiple IT services or multiple customers. *See also* operational level agreement.

service level management

(*Service Design, Continual Service Improvement*) The **process** responsible for negotiating **service level agreements**, and ensuring that these are met. SLM is responsible for ensuring that all IT service management processes, **operational level agreements** and underpinning contracts are appropriate for the agreed service level targets. SLM monitors and reports on service levels, and holds regular customer reviews.

service lifecycle

An approach to IT service management that emphasizes the importance of coordination and control across the various **functions**, **processes** and systems necessary to manage the full lifecycle of

IT services. The service lifecycle approach considers the strategy, design, transition, operation and continuous improvement of IT services.

service operation

(*Service Operation*) A stage in the lifecycle of an IT service. Service operation includes a number of **processes** and **functions** and is the title of one of the core ITIL publications.

service pipeline

(*Service Strategy*) A database or structured document listing all IT services that are under consideration or development, but are not yet available to customers. The service pipeline provides a business view of possible future IT services and is part of the **service portfolio** that is not normally published to customers.

service portfolio

(*Service Strategy*) The complete set of services that are managed by a service provider. The service portfolio is used to manage the entire lifecycle of all services, and includes three categories: **service pipeline** (proposed or in development); **service catalogue** (live or available for deployment); and retired services.

service provisioning optimization

(*Service Strategy*) Analysing the finances and constraints of an IT service to decide if alternative approaches to delivering the service might reduce costs or improve quality.

service reporting

(*Continual Service Improvement*) The **process** responsible for producing and delivering reports of achievement and trends against service levels.

Service reporting should agree the format, content and frequency of reports with customers.

service strategy

(*Service Strategy*) The title of one of the core ITIL publications. Service strategy establishes an overall strategy for IT services and for IT service management.

service transition

(*Service Transition*) A stage in the lifecycle of an IT service. Service transition includes a number of **processes** and **functions** and is the title of one of the core ITIL publications.

service validation and testing

(*Service Transition*) The **process** responsible for validation and testing of a new or changed IT service. Service validation and testing ensures that the IT service matches its design specification and will meet the needs of the business.

service valuation

(*Service Strategy*) A measurement of the total cost of delivering an IT service, and the total value to the business of that IT service. Service valuation is used to help the business and the IT service provider agree on the value of the IT service.

super user

(*Service Operation*) A user who helps other users and assists in communication with the **service desk** or other parts of the IT service provider. Super users typically provide support for minor **incidents** and training.

value on investment

(*Continual Service Improvement*) A measurement of the expected benefit of an investment. VOI considers both financial and intangible benefits. *See also* return on investment.

variable cost dynamics

(*Service Strategy*) A technique used to understand how overall costs are affected by the many complex variable elements that contribute to the provision of IT services.

Index

Index